OK, Let's D

'One of the year's funniest books, this collection of essays
from Irish journalist Freyne is witty, wise and worth returning
to again and again' *i*, Books of the Year

'Funny and adorable' Nina Stibbe

'Funny, smart, soulful and sometimes devastating, this book shows
life in all its shades. It made me laugh and cry. Freyne catalogues
his own flaws with a disarming frankness, pays tribute to his friends
and family, and mourns those he has lost. Perhaps most movingly, this
book articulates the daily struggle to face our own vulnerabilities'
Emilie Pine, author of *Notes to Self*

'Exquisite . . . One of the funniest writers in Ireland' *Irish Examiner*

'Immensely readable, warm, human and very, very funny' *Irish Daily Star*

'Patrick Freyne has a distinct and enviable gift for storytelling, guiding
the reader into the tardis of his brilliant brain; from music and families
to society and loss. Full of humour and tenderness, this book is an
absolute JOY' Sinéad Gleeson, author of *Constellations*

'There are moments in these entries that can leave you creased with
laughter . . . Freyne's radar is precision-honed to find the madness
within the mundane' *Sunday Independent*

'Hilariously, painfully, Freynefully brilliant' Joseph O'Connor

'Whether he's writing about his childhood on a military base,
working in a kebab shop with a Nazi in his teens, playing in punk
bands in his twenties or grappling with the question of whether to
have children, Patrick Freyne is a writer of rare humour, depth
and humanity. These essays are a delight' Mark O'Connell, Baillie
Gifford Prize-winning author of *To Be a Machine*

'F*cking fantastic. Patrick is a brilliant writer' Blindboy Boatclub

'I don't know another writer who could balance poignancy and hilarity
with such grace . . . Goosebumps! Guffaws! It's got it all. I love this
book' Doireann Ní Ghríofa, author of *A Ghost in the Throat*

'More moving than I ever expected and somehow funnier than
I assumed' Emer McLysaght, *Irish Times* Best Books of 2020

'No one makes me laugh like Patrick Freyne' Paul Howard

'Pixies were loud-quiet-loud. Patrick Freyne is funny-sad-funny.
I really loved his new book' Ed O'Loughlin

'It's warm, it's funny, it's clever, it's really well written. It's too
short, and that is the biggest compliment you can give a book'
Ryan Tubridy, RTÉ Radio One

'Genuinely moving . . . [It] will evoke warmth in anyone
who isn't totally sociopathic' *Hot Press*

'A cracking, sad, funny, honest, brave and hilarious read' Liz Nugent

'His trademark wit and wry humour are in abundance
throughout . . . An absolute tonic for our times' *RTÉ Guide*

'Beautiful . . . I was expecting it to be warm, wry, charming,
absorbing – I did not expect to be sobbing my heart out at the
end of each essay. It's some of the most excellent writing on
grief and mental health I have EVER read. But it is incredibly
funny too' Daisy Buchanan

'Lovely . . . Very worth reading' Dara Ó Briain

'Freyne's thoroughly entertaining debut is a flash of warmth
and wit in the darkness' *Totally Dublin*

'Truly gorgeous and deserves to be read' Eithne Shortall

'A delightful insight into the mind of the hilarious
Patrick Freyne. Showing life in all its shades, there are tender
moments too' *Irish Country Magazine*

'Hilarious – like snigger-out-loud funny – also deeply moving
and original . . . Exceptional' Róisín Ingle

'Readers are sure to find themselves touched by
Freyne's writing . . . Delightful' *Journal.ie*

'So honest, so funny and, most importantly, 11 / 10 for
self-deprecation' Sarah Breen

ABOUT THE AUTHOR

Patrick Freyne spent most of his twenties trying to be a rock star before
turning to the much more stable and secure world of journalism. He is
a features writer at the *Irish Times*. *OK, Let's Do Your Stupid Idea* is his first
book.

OK, *Let's Do Your Stupid Idea*

Patrick Freyne

PENGUIN BOOKS

This book is for Paul Clancy and Barry Jordan, who are missed.

PENGUIN BOOKS

UK | USA | Canada | Ireland | Australia
India | New Zealand | South Africa

Penguin Books is part of the Penguin Random House group of companies
whose addresses can be found at global.penguinrandomhouse.com.

Penguin
Random House
UK

First published by Sandycove 2020
Published in Penguin Books 2021

001

Copyright © Patrick Freyne, 2020

The moral right of the author has been asserted

Printed and bound in Italy by Grafica Veneta S.p.A.

The authorized representative in the EEA is Penguin Random House Ireland,
Morrison Chambers, 32 Nassau Street, Dublin D02 YH68

A CIP catalogue record for this book is available from the British Library

ISBN: 978-0-241-99253-1

Contents

Preface

My friend Corncrake rings me. After some preamble about the events of the day, he says, 'I read the story you sent me.'

'Oh,' I say.

'It's very well written,' he says.

'Thank you.'

'But.' Here it comes. 'I'm not sure who's going to read this.'

'Why?'

'Well, it's just about your life,' he says. 'It kind of feels like stuff you should be telling a counsellor, really.'

'Oh.'

'I mean, it's stuff that happens to everyone,' he says.

'OK.'

'If I was going to read a book about someone's life, it would be someone like Julius Caesar, or Napoleon, or some famous general.'

'Julius Caesar, Napoleon, or some famous general.'

'It's very well written,' he says again (he likes to be encouraging).

'You know there's a whole genre of work that's basically memoir writing,' I say. 'People who aren't particularly famous writing about their lives.'

'*Really?*'

'Even twentysomethings write memoir-essays now,' I say. 'It's a very popular genre.'

'*Really?* Are you sure?'

'I'm sure.'

'*Twentysomethings?* That sounds kind of stupid. Are you sure?'

It does sound kind of stupid now that I've said it out loud. 'I'm sure.'

There's a long pause. 'Well, you'd know better than me.' And then, 'It *is* very well written.'

'But you'd prefer if it was about Julius Caesar.'

There's a pause. 'Or Napoleon, or some famous general.'

'Thanks for your feedback,' I say, coldly.

'No problem,' he says, cheerfully.

It's the Military Life for Me

'Every man thinks meanly of himself for not
having been a soldier.'
— Samuel Johnson

When I was twelve years old, my army man father brought me on what I took to be a bonding father/son camping trip in a stretch of the Wicklow mountains. My mother drove us to the edge of civilization, where we got out of the car and walked up a dirt track. Along the way, my father cut and carved two walking sticks out of blackthorn branches and, after a few hours of walking, we camped in the shade of a wood by what I can only describe as a babbling brook, because it was a brook and it babbled.

It was idyllic, really. We ate army rations of sausages and beans from little foil tins heated over a campfire and, from time to time, I spoke coordinates that my father called out to me into a little walkie-talkie. Around twenty years later, the family was waxing nostalgic about this over after-dinner drinks.

'Why did we have a walkie-talkie?' I asked. It was a strange part of the memory that never quite made sense.

'Well,' said my father. 'We needed it to keep in touch with the rest of the men.'

'The rest of the men?' I said. 'I don't understand.'

'You see, there were rumours of an IRA training camp in the mountains and the Rangers had been asked to investigate,' said my father. The Rangers, by the way, were a crack commando squad and my dad was, at this time, their commanding officer.

'Right,' I said.

'I figured the terrorists would have their eyes peeled for guards and soldiers.'

'Sure.'

'But if they saw a man and a child, they'd think it was just a father and son on a camping trip.'

'I thought we *were* a father and son on a camping trip.'

'Oh no,' said my father. 'That was just a cover.'

'A cover?'

'Well, you were really my son,' admitted my father.

'I'm glad to hear it,' I said.

'But we weren't purely on a father-and-son camping trip,' he said.

'No,' I said, a little bitterly, 'apparently we were tracking terrorists.'

My father nodded happily.

'Was it not a bit dangerous?' asked my wife. 'What if you'd actually run into trouble?'

'Oh, we were *fine*,' said my father. 'I was armed.'

'*You had a gun?!*' I said.

Again, my father nodded happily. 'In a shoulder holster.'

'What type of gun?' asked my wife, whose hippy parents wouldn't let her play with toy guns and who will certainly, as a consequence, end up killing someone with a gun.

I didn't wait for an answer. 'I could have been *killed*!' I cried.

'But nothing happened,' said my wife, and, looking at my father, 'Right?'

'Nothing happened,' said my father, but he had a mysterious look on his face that led me to picture him drowning an IRA man in the brook as twelve-year-old me slept soundly nearby. I wouldn't put it past him.

'I'd like to say,' said my mother, 'that I had no idea this was going on.'

For a while there my siblings and I called my mother Carmella, after Carmella Soprano. She often, in retrospect, turns out conveniently not to have had any idea what was going on when we were younger. In reality, I suspect that, like Carmella Soprano, she could quite capably run my father's enterprises if left to her own devices.

In this instance – child-inclusive counter-terrorism – she was probably pleased to have a quiet house for the weekend and thought the off-chance her son might be involved in a paramilitary gunfight was a risk worth taking. Childcare standards were different in the 1980s, as people repeatedly remind me. There was no helicopter parenting back then, unless my father was planning to call in a helicopter gunship for back-up. But no, apparently, the Ranger wing didn't have access to a helicopter gunship at this time. I asked.

I shouldn't have been too surprised by all this. I had a

3

militarized childhood. When I was a boy my mother and father and my younger sister and brother moved to the Curragh Camp. This was the main training centre for the Irish army, a nineteenth-century base built by the British out of red bricks on a mineral-rich glacial plain. Queen Victoria inspected the troops there in 1861, but sixty years after independence it was filled with Irish soldiers and their families. There was a big water tower, two churches for two denominations, a just-short-of-Olympic-length swimming pool, an old red-brick hospital, a cinema where I saw *Jaws 3D*, many now-ornamental rusted-up tanks and seven army barracks, renamed after handover from the British in honour of the signatories of the 1916 Proclamation.

Soldiers lived in barracks dormitories, terraced houses and new estates on the edge of the camp. Officers lived in bigger, grander houses. As an officer's family, we lived in a red-brick, four-bedroom house with lino floors, a big Aga stove in the kitchen, bats in the chimney and no central heating. This was, sadly, in an era before Aga stoves were considered chic, before bats in the chimney were considered chic and when having central heating was considered very chic indeed.

Some of the officers' houses were bigger than others. One family lived in a seven-bedroom house so big that it had servants' quarters and a separate servants' stairs. Even then, I thought that if I ever had a house with servants' quarters it would be a shame not to get a few servants to go with it. That particular family did not have servants, which I thought showed a failure of imagination.

I didn't have friends for a significant period after we moved to the Curragh Camp and spent my days cycling around by myself, climbing over the old, rusted machines and getting into derelict buildings to loot any defunct military equipment I could find. I would collect bullet shells on the firing ranges and had plastic bags full of them in my wardrobe. I was so lonely I once ignored the red warning flags that indicated the firing range was in use, in order to keep walking towards a frantically waving out-of-breath soldier. The shocking thing about this for some of my angry neighbours was that a number of younger children followed after me. Lion cubs led by a donkey.

I think my mother felt similarly out of place when we lived there. Our household had a copy of *The Second Sex*, and my father and mother shared the breadwinning, cooking and cleaning duties. My dad might have been capable of killing a man with his bare hands, but he could also make an excellent queen cake with the same bare hands (and he probably even washed them in between). Meanwhile, my mother discovered that army wives were referred to in correspondence by their husband's rank, and many didn't have bank accounts and spent their lives being perpetual dinner-party hostesses.

Her closest friend in the Curragh was once a contestant in the Calor Kosangas Housewife of the Year competition, a televised celebration of social norms overseen by Gay Byrne. On this programme, my mother's friend cooked a quiche that really impressed Gay. She later won a bright yellow Citroën for being the Best Dressed Lady at the Galway Races.

The car was cool. It had a roof you could peel back. Going by her quiche, I suspect she would be CTO of Facebook if she had been born a few decades later.

There was a lot about the Curragh that seemed out of time. Some of the officers affected the aesthetics of the British Empire, with handlebar moustaches, cravats and pipes. On sunny days riding my bike around the camp I could see them outside the various officers' messes smoking their pipes, drinking brandy, practising their vowel sounds and reading English newspapers. Unlike some of the other residents of County Kildare, they hated the IRA, not just because of their empire fantasies but also because republican paramilitaries created a lot work for them. They seemed kind of lazy.

I recently asked my dad if I'd imagined this Raj-like atmosphere in the Curragh Camp. He, a workaholic, just sighed sadly. I had not imagined it. 'Everyone got a half-day on Wednesdays,' he said. 'But if you were in the golf club you also got another half-day on Friday.'

Dad was not in the golf club. He was in the aforementioned Ranger Wing, a commando unit tasked with keeping Ireland safe from paramilitarism and anarchy. As a young boy, I would sometimes cycle into their top-secret hideout to see what he was up to. 'Hello, Patrick!' the armed guards would say, never once checking if I was strapped with explosives or infected with cholera.

Most of the time, what my father was up to was abseiling out of a window or jumping from a helicopter into the Irish Sea, or doing something classified up at the Northern Irish border. Being a Ranger seemed like great fun.

Dad had special badges indicating he was a marksman and a paratrooper. Once he brought my cousin John and me to fire a gun out in one of the Curragh's many firing ranges. I shot my clip of ammunition one by one at a disappointingly abstract non-humanoid target a few hundred yards away. John, who loved America and hated communism, realized that it was a semi-automatic gun, flipped some switch and fired all of his bullets in one blast: 'Die, commies!'

I watched with envy and regret. I had been too cautious and I regretted it for years. John, by the way, is now a socialist hip-hop fan who hates imperialistic American foreign policy.

Dad was tough. I'd sometimes meet him when I was cycling around the edges of the camp as he was leading a march of exhausted soldiers all the way from the Glen of Imaal on foot. One weekend he came home from some training manoeuvres with a bad cut on his forehead from a stun grenade. I boasted about it for weeks. 'My dad was blown up by a grenade,' I said to the boys at school, whose boring dads worked at desks and had not been blown up by a grenade.

He once told me the story of a youthful military exercise up in the mountains, during which several men were tasked with evading the surveillance of others. One man broke his leg early on and yet still methodically evaded capture, or, if you want to be pedantic about it, *rescue*, for twenty-four hours. 'He wasn't very bright,' said Dad.

Dad had also faced more genuine dangers. As a young man he served in Cyprus with the UN, forming a bulwark between warring Turkish and Greek factions. He told me a story once about an officer having a gun pointed to his head by a commander from one of the factions. The officer said, 'You can shoot me, but then my men will just shoot you.' When I think of this now, I instinctively feel sad because I know I'll never get to say a sentence like that in the course of my work.

'Have you ever killed a man?' I asked once.

'No,' he said.

'Not even someone who deserved it?' I asked.

'No,' he said.

'Aw,' I said.

I really did say 'aw'. Even now, part of me wishes I could tell you that my dad has killed a man, but this is not the case. My dad hasn't killed even one measly person.

Nonetheless, he was really good at being an army man and to this day I meet towering, crop-haired taxi-drivers and barmen who served with him and have the height of admiration for him over and above other namby-pamby officers that they've known. 'Your dad was a tough man,' they tell me, shaking their heads in wonder.

'Tough but fair,' they always add, which makes me picture him punching them in the nose but then giving them an appreciative pat on the head. I imagine their assessment of me would be similarly pointed – 'weak but unfair' maybe, or 'fey hobo' possibly, or 'degenerate clown person'. They tend not to give their assessment of me, to be honest with you.

Of course, I wanted to be in the army back then. For a long time, I just assumed it was my destiny, and from a very young age I hoped there would be a nice big war to get stuck into before my time on Earth was done. As children, we played war all the time, which is another way of saying we played 'murder'. Small boys don't act out 'pestilence' or 'famine'. That would be distasteful. Militarized mass murder, on the other hand? Sure. That's healthy. Boys will be boys.

I had an advantage when it came to playing murder because my house was filled with army-surplus gear – helmets, water canteens, gas masks and bandoliers that had come from my pillaging of old buildings in the Curragh Camp or the largesse of my dad. My moral compass at the time was set by British war comics like *Victor* and *Battle*, in which various race and class stereotypes – gritty cockney sergeants, stiff-upper-lipped officers and gum-chewing Yanks – fought a version of the Nazis whose main failing was expansionism, wearing monocles and being a bit foreign. I don't remember any mention of the Holocaust in these comics.

They had a big impact on me. Father Duggan would come once a week to my primary school to teach us the finer points of Catholic doctrine, and I would quibble with him about what was morally acceptable in the field of battle.

'Thou shalt not kill,' he said, which seemed a bit extreme to me.

'What if there's a terrorist holding hostages in a cable car and he's got his finger on a detonator and the only way to stop him setting the bomb off is to shoot his head off?' I asked.

'That's probably OK,' he said, 'but you'd have to go to confession afterwards.'

'What if there were three enemy soldiers shooting at you and you could technically disarm them by shooting them in the legs but it would be safer for innocent bystanders to just shoot their heads off?' I asked.

'You should shoot them in the legs,' he said, though he didn't sound sure of it.

'What if you have a murderer at your mercy because he's surrendered, but you suspect he will escape and kill again?' I asked. 'Couldn't you just shoot his head off?'

'That would be right out,' said Father Duggan firmly. I was disgusted.

In retrospect, I'm slightly touched that Father Duggan didn't take the obvious tack and say, 'What are you talking about, Freyne? You don't have the skills to shoot a distant terrorist in the head. Why not restrict your moral quandaries to something you could conceivably do, like eating your sister's sweets or snitching on your friends?' Instead, he really tried to engage with me and, in the process, we imagined up the Gospel according to Andy McNab. 'Think of Jesus as the leader of the commandos,' he said to me once.

I liked Father Duggan, but I was very disappointed by his pacifist attitude. I wanted to be able to kill people without going to hell. Not all people. Just bad people. Like the Germans and the Japanese and possibly the Russians, depending on the war. He later left the priesthood to get married and so no longer had to deal with Jesuitical army brats like me. He was well out of it.

Children are psychopaths. I know and love many of them,

but at least half of them would stick me with a sharpened toothbrush if it meant they could get a really cool box of Lego. My most vivid memory of childhood war games are not what you'd now call 'healthy'. I remember emerging from a friend's house once only to discover that a barrage of youngsters had gathered on the green across the road (actually an unfinished building site) in order to 'get' my friend. 'Getting' people was a bit of thing when I was a boy. And there they all were, crouching behind discarded diggers and rusting barrels and unfinished ditches, ready to throw clods of dirt at my friend and his house.

The scenario played out much like one of the many Westerns I had seen.

'We've got you surrounded!' shouted a bigger boy as my friend and I cowered behind his garden wall.

'I'm here too!' I shouted.

'We're not here for you!' shouted the bigger boy. 'You're fine.'

'Really?' I shouted back.

'Yeah,' shouted the bigger boy. 'You should join us. We're only here to get *him*.'

If I had paid more attention to the tales of frontier heroism I'd watched, I would, at that point, have turned to my friend, put my hand on his shoulder, and said, 'I will never betray you,' and then sacrificed myself in some way. Instead, I turned to him, shook his hand in a 'no hard feelings' sort of way (I pictured myself as a young David Niven), and then hopped over the wall and joined the others behind their rusty barricades. This was my first act of betrayal. I remember standing there holding my clod of throwing dirt (I'd picked one up in order to fit in), contemplating the fickleness of fate and realizing, with horror, that my childhood was over. I was around six.

About seven years later I was introduced to a game called Prisoners of War by two strangers who turned up in a small wood of scraggly trees and briars at the edge of our housing estate in Newbridge, where we had recently moved. These were older boys and they wore the uniforms of the FCA, the Irish army reserve force. The FCA, from what I've gathered over the years, was where the state put teenage sociopaths before they started referring them to psychologists. One of the boys was big and lumpy with a thin moustache and a beret and mirrored sunglasses. The other was smaller and wirier with a similarly thin moustache and a bandana wrapped around his head. They both twirled hunting knives (there was a vogue for collecting these at the time – I knew a young entrepreneur at school who sold both hunting knives and scented erasers from his locker). News of the interlopers went around our housing estate and soon a dozen boys and girls were gathered around them in a clearing in the trees. They were here, they said, to 'train' us. And sure, it was summer, what else did we have to do?

The smaller boy stabbed open a can of beans with a knife and then ate them 'raw', which impressed us no end. Then the bigger one pointed at one hapless youngster and told him to run. The boy sped off across the field in front of us. The bigger boy casually picked up a bit of a tree branch and fired it after him so that it twirled through the air before clobbering him on the head and knocking him over, rendering him unconscious for a moment, disoriented for hours and arguably – I've met him since – confused for a lifetime. We all actually clapped at this point.

The boys drilled us for an hour or so, getting us to run through 'obstacle courses' (thickets filled with nettles) before explaining the rules of Prisoners of War. These were simple enough. We would run across the fields ahead of us, fields that were filled with trees and ditches and disused farm buildings and bizarre drainage tunnels, and then they would follow us and, one by one, catch us, beat us, then bring us back to the little wood and tie us to a tree with a scratchy blue rope. We all looked at one another. Yes, we were all thinking the same thing: *this sounds amazing.*

We played Prisoners of War every day for a while. After the customary speechifying and military exercises that started the morning (the bigger boy was a bit of a Patton-esque blowhard) we would all make our way across the fields, trying to find places to hide as the young psychopaths counted to sixty aloud.

Sometimes you'd go to a beloved hiding space in an old sewage pipe or beneath some corrugated iron only to find someone else already there. Sometimes *you* were the person already there, which was gratifying when some other poor child was caught in your vicinity. 'This is like real war,' you'd think, observing from behind a collapsed shed as teenage thugs thumped one of your neighbours.

If you were caught early in the day, you might get a punch in the head, and then you'd find yourself back in the scraggly woods being tied to an old, dead tree. They only had one big long rope, so every time they brought a new child back they had to untie everyone who was already imprisoned, then introduce a new child to the situation, before tying everyone up again. In retrospect, we were very cooperative. I don't think we were particularly well tied to that tree and I'm sure that we could have extricated ourselves if we'd wanted to. But that never occurred to us. Instead we would laze there for hours, chewing stems of grass and having philosophical conversations with other young people about our teachers and parents and the nature of reality. War really makes you think.

If you succeeded in hiding for a few hours and weren't tied to a tree, you missed the prisoners' scintillating conversation, but you got to enjoy the heightened fight-or-flight hormones coursing through your body as you heard the militarized teens beating through the bushes and getting angrier and angrier. When you were caught, you would receive what the older boy called a 'light beating' and would be brought back to the rotting tree, where your peers would give you a round of applause, and then everyone would go home to their nice middle-class homes, where the subject of mysterious bruises and teenage sadists in military gear was never mentioned. I think these were among the best weeks of my life.

In retrospect, I think I wanted to be in an army because I deeply wanted to fit in, and the idea of having rules to follow and a uniformed gang to be part of seemed like a great antidote to the clamour of fear and guilt and doubt that was already raging in my chest. I was, I guess, one of nature's fascists.

In my teenage years I worked out that I probably wouldn't fare too well in a war. The guy I could relate to best in the film *Platoon* was the one who survived by cowering behind some corpses. I also had a changing relationship to 'the rules'. I was no longer the type of person who would stay happily tied to a tree just because an unhinged person in a camouflaged jacket had asked me to. When there were clear-cut guidelines in life around who was the toughest or the fastest or the smartest or the prettiest, I now knew I wouldn't necessarily win. And that's when I realized that art was a better bet for me than sport or soldiering. With art, you could win in your own way. You could steal the lime-light. You could cheat.

This is obviously a personality flaw. I realized this over a decade ago, when explaining to my then soon-to-be wife why I didn't want a flashy wedding. 'I prefer people noticing me when it's least expected,' I said. 'Like when I sing at *someone else's* wedding. I like to "dance out of the shadows".'

Even as I said this, I knew there was something deeply wrong with me. Henceforth, 'dancing out of the shadows' became code for me stealing someone's thunder. And, to be fair, I 'dance out of the shadows' frequently to high praise. I'm an undercover show-off. Most of you other show-offs do it really badly. It's generally best to pretend to be reluctantly exposing your genius as an offhand favour. You can't quite do this as a football player or a military marksman.

Nobody apart from my wife has noticed my technique,

I think, and I know I'm ruining it for myself by mentioning it here. But I'm sorry. I can't help it. My favourite way to shine is playing by my own rules and on your special day.

In the 1990s, with this morally suspect new worldview already in place but not yet articulated clearly, I left thoughts of a military adulthood behind and started to plan my future as a novelist/musician/comic-book artist/commune-dwelling art punk. I still wanted to conform and belong, but I realized at this point that starting a band was a much better way of doing this than joining the army.

My dad didn't mind. He was, as I have pointed out, tough but fair and, if you were related to him, he was kind and loving. He may have been inclined to bring his elder son along on counter-terroristic sting operations, but he was never the autocratic military father of lore. In fact, I'd go so far as to say that my father's blend of maternal softness in the home and military hardness outside it was a pretty complex model of masculinity by the standards of the time.

And as both of his sons veered away from sport, militarization and any sense of practicality, he just accepted us for the unathletic, scene-stealing showboaters we were, eventually pinning his hopes for toughness on his grandsons and granddaughter, who by the age of three were wandering by us in army gear and football jerseys, clutching working drills in their chubby mitts.

'You never let us do that when we were small!' I complained.

'I wouldn't let you do that *now*,' he said.

I still have a lingering affection for the army and for the

Curragh Camp. Nowadays, when I look at myself and my acquaintances from journalism and music and literature, I lament our vagueness and angst and lack of discipline. None of us looks like we've ever punched an insurgent in the face. We're all so slumped and shaggy and floppy. A military bearing is a real thing and my father has it. When I introduced him to an author who'd spent a lot of time with the US army, the author instantly said: 'You're a military man, right?' Because of course he is. His hair is cropped, his back is straight and he walks with a marching confidence that most of us lack. I can recognize my dad's footsteps a corridor away. They're evenly paced. They're solid and definitive and reassuring. They cut through the noise of other people and other things. They tell me that help is at hand and that I don't need to worry.

The Thing about Me is, I Hate Drama

(A series of dubious things I did as a child)

When I was two and a half years old, I kicked a Yorkshire terrier named Squeaky. Squeaky was owned by Mrs R, an elderly family friend. I have no clear memory of this event, but the tale of me kicking Squeaky was infamous in my family for a while. My father says that Squeaky had it coming. Nobody liked Squeaky, he says. He got underfoot and he squeaked. But Mrs R was appalled. 'That child will come to no good,' she said. Now, I don't remember the specifics of kicking Squeaky, but I have a vague, shameful memory that it felt good.

My *earliest* memory is of straining to get out of a car seat. In my memory I am screaming, absolutely appalled to be so restricted. It's more a memory of a feeling than a memory of an event. If my rage could be given expression in language, it would be the sentence 'Let me out of here, ye pricks!' In retrospect, I'm surprised my parents even had a car seat. The standard way to transport children in those days was to leave them loose and plentiful in a hatchback. Nowadays, they're all strapped in and buckled up like Hannibal Lecter. According to this memory, however, my parents were ahead of the game when it came to child restraint and I resented it, loudly.

*

When I was three, I was taken to visit some distant family friends who had two daughters around my age. I was, for reasons too complex to go into, wearing a dressing gown, wellingtons and a bucket hat with a map of Australia on it. '*I'm* here!' I said, stressing the first syllable, standing in the doorway of their kitchen, my legs akimbo, my hands on my hips. 'It's *me*!' I added, stressing the last syllable. Then I jumped on a little plastic digger and pedalled furiously around the room. Everyone was very impressed, if I remember correctly.

A short time later, I chased a boy with a stick because he laughed at my Australia-themed bucket hat. I was sitting on top of an old and rusting digger – a real one – that had been left on the green across from our home after the builder had abandoned the estate and run away with everyone's money. I liked to pretend I was driving this digger and it had never occurred to me before that my Australia-themed bucket hat was anything other than fascinating. So, when the other, older and bigger boy laughed at me, saying something like, 'Look at you with your stupid hat' or 'The hat on you, you hat fool!' a red mist fell over my child-eyes, I picked up a bit of a tree branch and I chased the boy up the road while waving the branch over my head. My mother says she had never seen my father look so proud as he was that day, the day he got to see his son, rabid with infant rage, swinging a tree branch while chasing a bigger boy up the street for laughing at his hat. He told this story for years. It's only in retrospect, really, that I feel like I could have handled the situation better.

*

When I was four, I liked to talk to the little girl next door as though we were both in a remake of *Brief Encounter* (there were a lot of black-and-white matinees on the telly in those days). 'At last we're alone,' I'd say whenever her smaller sister waddled out of the room. I might have even called her 'darling'. And then I jumped into a pedal car and pedalled furiously around the yard. Everyone was very impressed, if I remember correctly.

When I was four and a half, my neighbour Mrs B collected me and some other local children from school, then stopped at the shops, got involved in a bit of a conversation with some people and left me for too long in the car. I was an impatient young man with things to do. I decided to abandon her car and walk home on my own. My fellow infants were appalled by my maverick ways.

'But you'll get lost!' said one wide-eyed urchin.

'I know the way,' I said. I was four and a half. I was pretty sure I knew the way and not for the last time I discovered that I was right and was excessively pleased about it.

Unfortunately, I left Mrs B with the impression that she had mislaid a child. Terrified and contrite, she sped in her little car right up to our door, trying to find a way to tell my parents the bad news.

Her terror and contrition evaporated when she saw my mother trying to coax me off the garage roof. At that time my mother and I regularly had differences of opinion. One of these differences of opinion was about whether a small child should be on top of the garage roof and it was this difference of opinion that was being ventilated when Mrs B came up the driveway. My mortified mother says she could see Mrs B's mood changing before her eyes.

'That child will come to no good,' said Mrs B.

'She really said that?' I asked my mother, many years later.

'Well, not exactly,' said my mother, 'but I could see she was thinking it.'

When I was five, I married my cousin. Sort of. I had melodramatic tendencies at this point in my life, so the first time I stayed overnight away from my parents at my cousins' house, I decided, as dusk fell, to go all quiet and brooding and contemplate my tragic separation from my progenitors. I saw smoke in the distance and said, 'That could be my house. My house could be on fire. My parents could be dead already.' Then I swivelled my head dramatically in my cousins' direction: 'Will I ever see my parents again?'

So my cousin Naoimh, who brooked no nonsense, decided to distract me by marrying me off to my younger cousin, Aisling. Naoimh is an innovator and she liked to oversee marriage ceremonies back then. Aisling was one day younger than me and I think Naoimh figured that, as we were the same age, we belonged together. The ceremony was quite elaborate. My youngest cousin, John, was a ring-bearer/ flower girl. I vaguely remember giving a speech. For a while I think we did this every time we visited each other's houses.

There's also a picture from around that time in which it appears that Aisling and I are running off together. My parents and aunts and uncles thought this was 'cute' because Catholicism had done a number on everyone in Ireland and an incestuous child marriage was a lot more appealing than divorce or rural depopulation. In the picture, I'm holding a brown leatherette suitcase and wearing stretched-out corduroys (I was a large child) and a rectangular velvet tea-cosy on my head that makes me look like a Cossack. Aisling, a smaller child with rosy red cheeks, is sitting astride the type of pedal tractor that was popular at the time and holding another suitcase. The picture is framed with the carelessness that was common in family albums back then. It looks like a picture that immigrants might have brought with them to America in the nineteenth century. We have very serious expressions on our faces and we look like we've been married for several decades. I recognize now that marrying your first cousin isn't permitted in Irish law, but 1979 was a different time.

When I was five and a half, on a visit to my grandparents' farm, I opened a gate and let a big grey snorting horse out of its field. I did it for the best reason there is: I wanted to see what would happen. What happened is this: the horse bolted by me and galloped down the lane into the far distance. Then my father and several of my uncles came running out of the pebble-dashed farmhouse and jumped in cars and chased it. I felt a little guilty. 'It just got out,' I said, unconvincingly. And then, wary that I might be losing control of the narrative, I decided that I was scared of the horse and I started to cry.

*

When I was six and my mother was babysitting the children of our neighbours, I thought it would be funny to run in and tell her that one of them – the smaller, less interesting one – had fallen into an exposed sewage tank across the green in our unfinished housing estate. My mother ran across the green in a panic. The girl was actually playing with dolls in our back garden. 'Surprise!' I said, when my mother discovered this.

'What were you thinking as you ran shrieking across the green?' I asked my mother some years later.

'I was thinking, "Oh God it would be better to lose one of my own."'

Fair enough, I thought. I was asking for that.

When I was seven, I used my booksmarts to ingratiate myself with the local youngsters in the County Kildare housing estate in which we found ourselves temporarily washed up. At this time I had many books about the Stone, Bronze and Iron ages, in which bearded semi-naked men could be seen extracting base metals from the earth in fully painted illustrations. This, I told my youthful neighbours, would help me to help them find gold in the field behind our houses. We went out into the field and gathered some stones. It was a rocky field. We cracked the stones open and saw some shiny quartz-like substance within.

'Is that gold?' they asked me.

'Yes,' I said, confidently.

'Are we rich?' asked the biggest neighbour.

'Yes,' I said. 'Let's find more.'

We continued our mining enterprise for a few days. Our base of operations was the garage of the boy whose home backed on to our supply of rocks. We even used it when their family went off on holidays.

'Are we allowed to be here?' asked the biggest neighbour.

'Yes,' I said, just assuming that we were allowed to be there. I mean, surely everyone could see that our mining enterprise was very, very important.

'Are we really allowed to be here?' asked the biggest neighbour a few days later as the householder's car pulled into the driveway.

'Maybe we're not,' I said, as, not for the first time in my life, real-time fact-checking destroyed a good story. We all leapt out of the garage into the back garden and over the wall.

At some point my peers realized that we were not going to get rich mining rocks in a field in Newbridge and that my claim to expertise was just a handful of books and a rich and authoritative voice (for a seven-year-old).

A few days later some boys put me into a shopping trolley and rolled me down the hill that led into our estate and towards a busy junction below. These events may not be related but in my head I just assumed this was what New-bridge people did to carpetbaggers and I resolved to leave town. We moved to the Curragh Camp shortly thereafter, presumably at my insistence. (Lest you think this book is written by the ghost of a 1980s child, I managed to overturn the trolley before it hit the traffic.)

*

When I was nine, I began to pretend that I liked sport. I did this in order to fit in and I did it for around seven years. The truth is I can barely comprehend sport's existence. Ten seconds into a sports game – and I mean *all* of the sports games, from archery to z-cars – I find my eyelids drooping and the colours on the screen blending into one another. It's like I have a sports-specific learning difficulty. However, as a child, I also had the instincts of a rural politician and I knew that not liking sports would be no good for my social standing as I moved from school to school.

So I collected football stickers and played on football and rugby teams and accompanied my friends to matches and memorized useful names, facts and phrases. I hated it so much. Let's face it, sport is just stupid. Nothing is created. No necessary tasks are completed. The costumes are no fun. The characters aren't that interesting. At the end of a game of sports, as far as I can see, a bunch of grunting people are just more tired than they were earlier in the day.

My only advantage as a sportsman was that I was large for my age, so, although I didn't have any interest in the games and I didn't have the skill to take the ball off anyone, my teammates discovered that if they put me in a defensive position, then occasionally I fell on someone at a convenient moment. They took to calling me 'Bonecrusher' after a time they momentarily thought I'd broken someone's leg (I'm sorry, Seamus, I was genuinely aiming for the ball). This nickname did not fit my more urbane self-image. I was living a lie, but it took me years to figure this out.

The filmmaker John Waters says that when a stranger

asks him what he thought of 'the game', he asks them what they thought of the most recent Strindberg production. In contrast, when a stranger asks me what I thought of the match, I stab them repeatedly in the throat with my best biro.

When I was around ten, my parents commissioned a picture of their three children from a professional photographer to mark my sister's first Holy Communion. This picture is on the stairway in my parents' house still and there is nothing holy about it.

Let me describe it. It's got that strange vague burnt brown and orange background that a lot of photography studios used in that era. My sister looks quite saintly in the picture. She is grinning a gap-toothed grin and wearing the man-dated white Catholic child-bride costume and she is holding a prayer book in her gloved hands. My younger brother, the happy simpleton, is seated on a chair beside her, beaming at the camera from beneath his shock of blond hair, wearing a blue and red T-shirt that bears the legend 'T-Shirt' in white script. (What ingenious literalist designed that T-shirt? I want to shake their hand.) I am standing behind my brother with my hands resting on his shoulders, ominously close to his throat. I am wearing a sensible V-neck and a shirt and tie and I look very stylish.

I wished that my stylishness was what people would focus on when viewing this picture. 'Look at how stylish Patrick is!' I hoped to hear them say. Instead their eyes would pass over the picture, after which they would do a double-take, and say, 'Oh my!'

This is because I have a deranged expression on my face that leaves anyone viewing the picture in no doubt that I intend to harm this child. My eyes are hooded, my teeth are bared and I am projecting my bottom jaw outward so as to give myself a thuggish underbite. Why, oh why, did my parents choose *this* photograph for prominent placement in the family home? Possibly it was the only one they had. Possibly all of the others from the shoot had even worse flaws. And possibly, just possibly, this was what my face actually looked like at that time and the next photos in the sequence feature an adult prising a fratricidal pre-teen off of his brother.

Best not dwell on it, I think.

When I was thirteen, my friend Corncrake figured our lives weren't exciting enough, so he made things up. For example, he called me McManus because, he said, 'I always wanted a friend named McManus.'

'My name isn't really McManus,' I found myself explaining to people he introduced me to.

He made up other things too, but he's asked me to remove them from this essay. They were right here in the text. So, imagine something terrible around about where this paragraph is. It's a measure of how *bad* these things were that he's fine with the next thing.

One day Corncrake paid a smaller child fifty pence to pull my tracksuit bottoms down while I was talking to a girl I really fancied. One moment I was impressing her with how good I was at interrupting her and the next moment my tracksuit was around my ankles. I did the only thing I could think of to save face: I chased the smaller child around the estate screaming, pulling my trousers up as I ran. When I caught and began to shake the terrified child, he revealed that Corncrake was his employer. So then I chased Corncrake around the estate for a while. I caught him and started shaking him up and down on a kerb shouting, 'Why? Why?' as he laughed. For some reason none of this redeemed me in the eyes of the girl I fancied. Corncrake is still my best friend.

When I was fifteen, I was in a school band, and I would deliberately learn complicated guitar chords just so I could put them in songs I was writing and then watch my friends struggle to play them. I wasn't very confident about my guitar-playing abilities and this made me feel better. The music I liked at the time was the smooth AOR sound of aging baby-boomers like Phil Collins, Dire Straits and Eric Clapton. Consequently, the first two songs I ever wrote were 'Skies of Blue (Will Never Die)', which was narrated by a slightly jaded older man musing about his lost youth and which included a complex A9 chord, and 'Honey (I Love You Still)', which was written from the perspective of a middle-aged man contemplating his long marriage and featured a difficult B7 chord. I was *fifteen*. As my songs had chords that required at least four fingers to play and words that required having alimony payments and prostate problems to understand, I wasn't in that band for very long.

When I was fifteen and a half, I discovered kissing. Sadly, the first three girls I kissed were all going out with the same boy at the time that I kissed them. He was an older boy who wore cowboy boots, rode a motorbike and had a mysterious collection of jangling keys on a keychain. As in most secondary schools, everyone in my school had their place. I was a member of a well-established 'nerd herd', but for a while slightly older popular girls liked to 'discover me', as if I were an obscure indie band. They'd metaphorically remove my spectacles and let my hair down like I was a prudish librarian in a Hollywood film. 'Why, Ms Havenstock, you're ravishing!' they would say, or something to that effect, and then there'd be momentary recognition of my hitherto hidden hunky qualities before I was returned to relative obscurity. Anyway, all of these girls were going out with the same boy.

The first time one of this boy's girlfriends kissed me, I didn't know she was his girlfriend. She was an older blond-haired girl I'd met in the Gaeltacht. (The Gaeltacht is basically teenage sex camp; a place where teenagers are sent to learn Irish but where, deprived of a language in which they are fluent, they snog each other instead.) This girl pretty much took me in hand and instructed me how to kiss her. I was a little shellshocked, to be honest. So was her boyfriend when he found out. At first, he made a bit of a joke about it. Then he sought me out to tell me how funny he found the joke. I pretended to find it funny too. I mean, I didn't really find it funny but I was relieved. I thought he was going to hit me.

The second girl I kissed happened to be this boy's next girlfriend. She was a friend of mine, but I didn't know she was going out with this boy until a rumour ran around the school that he was going to beat me up this time. It was the talk of the school. When he entered the fifth-year locker-room there was a silence and the room cleared. But he did not beat me up, because he wasn't really a violent kid. Instead he just gave me a stern talking-to. I took this solemnly because I definitely thought he was going to hit me. He was a good person really and I was apparently a bad thing that happened to good people. We parted as, if not friends, then two people who could safely assume they weren't going to kiss each other's girl-friends.

Six months later when I kissed his third girlfriend, I have to admit that I knew she was his girlfriend. I did think they were on a 'break' but I might have been deluding myself because she was amazing. This time when the rumour went around the school that he was going to beat me up I figured I really did deserve it. He didn't beat me up. He just stared at me with incomprehension and said, 'Why are you doing this?' and I said, honestly, '*I don't know.*'

I really didn't know. I was hardly a Lothario. From his perspective, it probably looked like I was trying to ruin his life. But I really wasn't. Not consciously. I think about him often and his plaintive '*Why are you doing this?*' And it makes me wonder if I've messed with him in any other way since that I might be unaware of. I think about everyone I've kissed in the decades that have passed and wonder about their con-nection to him. I mean, some days I look at my wife and wonder if she's secretly bigamistically married to him. If it is thus revealed, if I open the door one day and he is standing there with his boots and keys, a broken man once more, and he says, 'Why are you doing this?' I'll just think, 'OK, this makes sense.'

When I was sixteen, I stole some consecrated Holy Communion wafers. Even typing this now I feel shaky, and I haven't been a practising Catholic in decades. I mean, I quite like the Jesus of the Gospels, and he doesn't deserve to be so molested by snotty teens. I still maintain my friend made me do it.

At that stage in my life, my belief in God had wavered but I wouldn't have quite identified as an atheist. Going to Mass was just one more boring teenage obligation that I stoically accepted, like Irish class and pretending to like sports. I wasn't sure if I had a soul or if God existed or if there was a heaven or hell. I hadn't really considered my position philosophically until I met S and he forced me to.

S had a mess of backcombed raven-black hair and Doc Martens that came to his knees and a neck festooned with chains and crosses. He was so pale I'd describe him as light blue. He listened to punk bands like the Dead Kennedys who produced albums with sacrilegious titles like *Frankenchrist*. He educated me. He created an exquisitely detailed family tree of punk, painstakingly mapped out in black biro. (Because I am terrible at keeping track of things, I have, of course, lost it.) It clearly explained how all the genres and musical figures were related, and it suggested to me that when punk's anarchist revolution did arrive, S would be one of the bureaucrats recording every act of countercultural iconoclasm.

When we met we instantly bonded. I was attracted to his controlled and measured wildness and he instantly became a correctively bad influence on me. It's a little harder to see what attracted him to me, given that I was a slightly preppy, blazer-wearing nerd who, as I've already explained, really liked the smooth croonings of mid-eighties Phil Collins.

S and I bonded and collaborated over two things:

a) The creation of a pen-and-pencil comic-book epic about a post-apocalyptic punk revolution
b) a Jesus sandwich

I'm not entirely sure why S wanted to make a Jesus sandwich. I was never entirely convinced he really disbelieved in God. It was more like he just deeply disliked Him. He was thumbing his nose at Him, not quite denying His existence. As for me, it hadn't even occurred to me to be annoyed with God. I just wanted S to think I was cool, which, when I think about it now, is a far worse reason for being sacrilegious.

During the week we would spend our spare time scribbling and sketching our inky punk opus and then, at Mass, we would take part in a painstakingly orchestrated Christheist. We would go up the aisle to Communion looking ever so holy, then we would take the host in our hands under the good-natured eye of the priest, put it to our lips and pretend to swallow it while really keeping hold of it in our sweaty, sacrilegious palms. Then S would add them to a growing pile of, if you believe in transubstantiation, Jesus parts.

S still has our comic-book collaboration, but he does not have the Jesus sandwich because a slightly more pious teenager spotted us gloating heretically and ran to a teacher to blow the whistle. (I was always amazed at how quick religious kids were to tell on us; had they forgotten the eleventh commandment, 'Snitches get stitches'?)

This led to S having to 'dispose of the evidence' on a stairwell in school as we listened to angry voices bounding towards us. He did this by shoving a fistful of hosts into his mouth. Even as it was all happening, watching S's teeth and cheeks and throat dispose of Our Lord's soggy dough, I felt certain that the soul that I didn't quite believe in was destined for a hell that didn't necessarily exist. I feel the same certainty to this day.

Here, then, is a partial list of enemies I had made by the time I was sixteen:

The boy who laughed at my Australia-themed
    bucket hat
Mrs R and Mrs B
My mother
A horse who lived on my grandparents' farm
My happy simpleton brother
The child that Corncrake paid to pull my tracksuit
    bottoms down
Corncrake

A mob of Kildare urchins who I lied to about
    gold-prospecting
All the girls I tried to impress, except those who
    were going out with the boy with the jangling keys
The boy with the jangling keys
Squeaky, a small dog
Our Lord

Coolmountain

In 2005, when we were all grieving, we drove out to Coolmountain in West Cork, where, fifty years before, my
mother's family had loaded all their belongings on to a truck
and headed for a different life in Cork city.

We were in two cars. Some people were missing. My
grandmother and my mother's oldest sister, Marie, had died
within two months of each other a few months before and it
still felt raw. One of the cars contained my mother, her
younger sister, Phil, and my father. The other, my uncle
John's taxi, contained John, myself, John's grandson Josh
and my cousin, also called John.

You don't need to remember all these names. There are a
lot of Johns and names beginning with 'Jo' on my mother's
side of the family. My mother was christened Hannah but is
commonly called Joan. Both names, she says, are female
versions of John. She regularly has problems at passport control when her boarding pass and passport don't match and
this explanation doesn't always cut it.

As he drove his taxi through the sun-dappled hills of West
Cork, Uncle John told us a secret. He told us that his recently
deceased mother, my grandmother, had been pregnant with
Marie at the time of her wedding. After my grandmother's
death, he explained, they had come across her marriage cert.

The dates didn't quite add up. But that's all they knew. They don't know how this fact affected their mother and father's lives in the dark, shame-filled Ireland of the 1940s. They didn't know who else knew about it. They didn't know how well it had been hidden. They just knew it had been hidden. It would have been shocking then. It wasn't now.

'Joan won't be happy I told you,' said John, grinning widely. He had the warmest grin. He was still a handsome man.

We reached the dilapidated old schoolhouse where my mother and her siblings had been educated. As soon as my mother got out of the other car, I brought the secret up. I was probably self-righteously blasé about it.

'I didn't tell you only because I wasn't sure Nanny would want you to know,' said my mother.

'I don't think there's any reason for secrets any more,' said John, enjoying this a little too much. 'There's nothing to be ashamed of.'

'I agree,' said my mother, through slightly gritted teeth. 'But I didn't think it was our secret to tell.'

We pottered around the edges of the schoolhouse for a while. It was clad in corrugated iron and was rusted and overgrown with nettles and wildflowers. Through the windows you could see broken furniture, and there were holy pictures on the walls. It would be awful to have to live next door to, but it was a beautiful thing to visit.

The quality of the light in Coolmountain is strange. It seems to shimmer above the rocky, sparsely wooded hills as though it were bound to them. The effect is supernatural. It feels as if every corner you turn brings you into a lost valley.

It's peculiar and spectacular and disorienting. The scale of everything is strange and the horizon seems perpetually hazy. It all feels very remote indeed, despite being not much more than an hour's drive from Cork city.

After my mother and her family left this area, there was an influx of British and German hippies to the more isolated parts of West Cork. There had been a German newspaper article, apparently, suggesting that the south of Ireland would be one of the safest places to be in the event of a nuclear war. The fallout would avoid the place, the way the tax inspectors did. The hippies seem to be largely gone now, but if you drive up those dark, narrow, tree-cluttered roads to have a look, you'll see that the hillsides near my family's old farm are filled with jerry-rigged cabins and huts built from what looks like salvaged rubbish. They're cluttered with solar panels and water tanks and caravans and over-grown vegetable patches and German letterboxes.

In the 1980s and 1990s my grandfather became con-vinced, whenever the family visited the old farm, that the hippies were growing marijuana in their rickety green-houses. His more worldly, lightly bohemian children scoffed at this: 'It's just tomatoes,' they said. Later, when there was a cannabis haul close to the farm, they had to admit that he was right. The hippies were growing drugs on what locals called, for a while, Hash Mountain.

We got back into the cars and drove up the tiny, winding roads to the old farmhouse in Clogher where the family once lived. The hedgerows scratched the sides of the cars and my uncle told us stories about my grandmother's brothers. They were in construction and they were quite wealthy. They were known sometimes as the Demolition O'Mahonys, and sometimes as the Gandhi Mahonys because of the bespectacled, bald appearance of my great-grandfather. They made and lost fortunes in the byways of West Cork. My grandmother worshipped them and did whatever they said. A couple of them controlled the less well-off relatives, checked the provenance of people who wanted to marry into the family and generally stood back watching everyone in glowering judgement.

'They sound like hard work,' I said, once we were out of the car and standing in the yard.

'You have no idea,' said Uncle John.

'Ah, there was a lot of kindness in them as well,' said my mother.

My mother's old home is unrecognizable from what it was when they lived there. Subsequent owners had enlarged it with various not quite up-to-code extensions. Tom Barry and his men had hidden here during the War of Independence. And here is where my grandmother would read to her children from Barry's memoir and from books by the Brontës. She never went beyond primary school, but she loved literature. She could recite chunks of Goldsmith's *The Deserted Village* from memory. Members of my mother's family came back here a lot in later years, John more than the rest. He didn't believe in God, but Coolmountain had become a sort of holy place for him.

'I don't know how anyone made a living here,' said my father, who comes from good farming land in Kilkenny.

'We barely made a living,' said Phil, and her siblings laughed.

My mother pointed out the route she used to take to school, clutching Marie's schoolbag as she walked. As a child, my mother never looked up when addressed by an adult. Marie spoke for her. Marie looked after her. When I was a child, I had no doubt that if anything happened to my parents, Marie would look after me too. While the others went to college, Marie went out to work. She loaned a month of her hairdresser's salary to one of the Demolition O'Mahonys when he was between fortunes and she was still in her teens. She looked after people. She sometimes needed looking after herself, first as a child when she had to have an operation on her brain and lost the sight in one eye, and later as an adult when the cancer that took her breast metastasized without anyone noticing. This breaks my heart.

My mother and her siblings thought about this place, dreamt about it and longed for it after the family moved to Cork city. When I was young, my mother told us stories that made life in Coolmountain sound like an idyllic adventure. She talked about wandering the fields and running past haunted cottages and a day when she tricked John into clambering on top of an uncooperative bullock. As we got older, her stories conveyed more of the hardship of their lives. They were subsistence farmers with no electricity, cooking on an open fire.

Because my generation of the family are spoiled rotten, we regularly teased them. 'I suppose you remember the first time you saw white bread?' I said.

'Yes!' said my mother. 'We were amazed.'

They never quite made the farm work. My grandfather

39

was not always well. He had Parkinson's disease towards the end of his life, but he also suffered from something else. When his children were young, he would become paranoid and withdrawn and would retreat from the family. When he was particularly bad his sister would be called and then the family would take him away to get shock therapy. It wasn't easy on them. It hurts them to remember it. My mother says that her father was so distant she sometimes wondered what he felt about them. One time when he came back from hospital, his hair greyer, he walked towards them laughing and my mother thought, 'Maybe he does love us after all.'

In the early 1960s my grandfather was offered a job by the nuns who ran an old folks' home in Montenotte, where the rich people of Cork lived, overlooking the harbour. He was to manage a small farm for them. They had a gate lodge for his family to move into, and my grandmother and mother took a trip to the city to have a look at it. Afterwards, my grandmother went to the little chapel and prayed and wept with relief and happiness while my mother watched. 'She always wanted to be a city person,' my mother said.

When it was time to move, they loaded up a red Bedford truck owned by a relative and drove into the city. They looked, says my aunt Phil, 'like the Beverly Hillbillies'. The children had to sit under a tarpaulin in the back with all their belongings, and my grandfather cried when saying goodbye to his horse.

In Cork, they struggled at first to fit in. They weren't just moving from the countryside to the city. In a lot of ways they were moving from the nineteenth century to the twentieth. They knew nothing about pop music or fashion. In one of the few surviving photographs of the children, the girls are wearing huge bows in their hair. In the country, they'd cooked on an open fire and read by lamplight. In their new home, they listened to The Beatles and discovered cinema and whole shops filled with books.

But as we stood there that day in Coolmountain, the sun glinting off the leaves and swallows diving down the roads between the hedgerows, you'd wonder why anyone would ever want to leave.

I know a bit about what it's like to live in the shadow of another place. When I was six, we moved from a suburb of Cork city to the army base in County Kildare where my father worked. Cork was home to this extended family of beloved cousins and aunts and uncles and, also, the emotional mythology of Coolmountain. Our new home felt empty.

In the late 1990s I started to visit Cork city more regularly, largely because I was touring with my band by then. I once made the mistake of saying, from the stage of the rock venue Nancy Spains, 'I used to be from Cork.'

'You're always from Cork, boy!' yelled a voice from the audience. It was Uncle John, never one to be afraid of shouting up at a performer. And he's right. I'll always be from Cork.

Cork city always feels a bit wilder and older and more informal than Dublin, where I live now, but this might be because when I was in a band we usually stayed in the various flats and houses my cousin John Casey rented across the city. As a child I called him Casey John, which made him sound like a character from some American folk ballad. He is the nicest man I know and his friends were a wild bunch. They had pictures of hunger-strikers on the walls and they played hip-hop and rebel songs on their stereo. Impromptu parties could start at any time. You might be lying asleep in a sleeping bag on their sitting-room floor and be woken at three in the morning because some stragglers had just arrived in from Sir Henry's, Cork's then-famous dance-music club, or because one of the flatmates had put a callout on the pirate-radio station they listened to. 'And here's another invite from the lads on the Wilton Road! Come on down if you want to get langered.' Or one of them might be sitting rolling a joint and he'd suddenly stick his head up as though hit by the Newtonian apple.

'We should have a game of hurling.'

'But it's freezing out.'

'We could have it . . .' Dramatic beat. 'Inside!'

In recent years, my mother and her sister Phil have spent a lot of time concerned with gravestones. First they wanted to get the name of their youngest sibling, Patrick Joseph, added to the family gravestone in St Oliver's cemetery in Cork City. He had died at birth owing to the mistakes of a drunk doctor, and my grandmother had had to stay in hospital for a while before returning home. My mother remembers the way Phil snuggled herself into her side at the sight of the sad-eyed woman who eventually appeared in the doorway. 'That's not a strange lady,' my mother told Phil. 'That's your mammy.'

She also remembers how a relative turned to her mother to admonish her. 'Don't be crying, gedleen,' she said, and then, my mother says, my grandmother stopped crying. They didn't see her mother cry over her lost baby or mention him again until she was in an old folks' home towards the end of her life.

The saddest words in Ireland are 'It was a different time.' Before she died, my grandmother had an intuition that things had changed in the world outside, and she began talking about her dead son. 'I don't want him to be forgotten,' she said. So before she died my mother and her sister made sure to get Patrick Joseph added to their father's gravestone. Patrick Joseph was a part of their life, after all. As children in Coolmountain they had prayed to him. Not *for* him, but *to* him. They felt he watched over them.

My grandmother, in her last years, also spoke about two sisters of hers who had died very young. She was the last of her large family alive, and few knew the sisters had ever existed, but my grandmother never forgot them. Lizzie had died as a baby. Kitty reached the age of seven.

Nowadays, early experiences of death are central to people's life stories and personal mythology. In those days there was just silence. When my mother and Phil eventually sourced a death certificate for Kitty, this aunt they had never met, it turned out that she had died of whooping cough. These children, these heartaches, were almost forgotten by history, but their names are now recorded in stone too.

*

After their mother and their sister died, Joan, Phil and John began meeting up more often. They always seemed young when they were together. They reverted to patterns of sibling teasing that I imagine started in childhood in the hills of West Cork. My self-employed uncle believed that his well-pensioned teacher sisters had notions. As the recession kicked in, he liked to imagine them scavenging through bins together. 'Oh, I've found a lovely sandwich, Phil!' he'd say in a parody of a posh Cork accent.

My mother and Phil would pretend to be annoyed. They would insist that it was public servants who held the country together while John would insist that the entire public sector was, in fact, a pile of cossetted leeches and that the true working man never got a fair shake. All the while he would drink cup after cup of black coffee.

He had a knack for letting the air out of your tyres.

'I've been playing your record in the taxi,' he said to me once.

'That's great!'

'Steady on, boy. Not everyone likes it. Sometimes they ask me to turn it off.'

I often thought that Joan, Phil and John were the cleverest people I knew. They managed to get university degrees despite their small-farm origins, and in the process they ended up encountering people far better off than they were. My mother recalls attending a meeting of the UCC Philosophical Society at which the socialist son of a doctor got a round of applause for asserting they did not want to 'turn out like our parents'.

'I couldn't understand it,' she says. 'All I could think of was how much I wanted to turn out like their parents.'

And they read a lot. They read feminist philosophers and banned books and historical doorstoppers. They did well, but if they had had their roots in the home of a Montenotte barrister rather than a subsistence farm in Coolmountain, I believe they could have ended up running the country. I think they suffered from a lack of confidence. They might have each suspected they were the smartest person in the room at different points in their lives, but they never *knew* it.

I come from them, and I obsessed over Cork, and they obsessed over Coolmountain. And so I feel a weird pull towards a place where I have never lived and have only visited half a dozen times. By the time I was twelve I had lived in seven different houses, so I think feeling drawn towards an ancestral homestead was a reasonable response. In my mind, our move from Cork echoed my mother's family's move from their farm. In fact, all of my life experiences feel like echoes of the lives lived by people with faces very like mine on a perpetually sunlit hilltop in West Cork.

One of my earliest memories is of being read to by my grandmother in her bedroom in Cork city very early in the morning. In my memory I was very young and she was trying to distract me from the fact that her husband, my grandfather, was outside the locked door pacing around the landing, clearly agitated. The handle of the door would turn occasionally. I couldn't make sense of this memory until I learned about my grandfather's mental-health issues.

'Does that sound like something to do with his illness?' I asked my mother, years later.

'Yes,' said my mother quietly.

She says I walk like him. When she sees me coming down a street, she says it's like she's looking at her father. An echo.

As well as a family homeplace and some family secrets, we have a family cancer. We learned about it first in 2003, when my mother was diagnosed. Several years later John was stricken with it too. The cancer my grandmother died of is a related strain – I checked. The illness my mother and John had is called CLL (chronic lymphocytic leukaemia) but, because both of them ended up with it, it's more specifically called familial CLL. There's a hereditary component to the familial variation, so this cancer could well be in the future for me or anyone else in my mother's family.

My mother has become a model of how to handle a chronic, incurable condition. She managed to work until retirement, keeping her mortal fears at bay, monitoring infections, keeping track of her medications and asking her doctor a lot of questions. (Always ask your doctor questions, by the way: it reminds them that you're a person and not just a collection of symptoms in a blue file.) My mother asks the politest, firmest questions.

When she was first diagnosed, the internet was not our friend. It suggested that she would live twelve years at the outside limit. I took this as a given and started to read books about bereavement and mourning. I read *The Year of Magical Thinking* by Joan Didion and thought, 'How true.' I dived into religious writings and tried not to cry when I saw grandmothers playing with their grandchildren. Meanwhile, my mother got on with things, manoeuvring herself around the medical system and still paying for me whenever we went out for dinner. In fact, a bit of carefulness and a bit of luck has meant that she has lived long enough to benefit from a new range of revolutionary drugs. She's still here sixteen years later. That feels like a miracle to me.

John wasn't so fortunate. Towards the end of his life he needed a lot of help from his sisters and his children. I think he worried them a lot. He would disobey doctor's orders and stand at the sidelines of football matches in the freezing winter and then ring them late at night in fits of fever. He grew thin and he grew frail. You could encircle his wrist with your thumb and forefinger, but he could still illuminate a room with his grin.

I think he was glad, when it came to it, to be surrounded by his children and all the other people who loved him in the safety of a hospital bed. A lot of people loved him, because he was supremely loveable. After he died, they put flowers on the chair where he sat outside his local café. It goes without saying that he shouldn't have been sitting out there in the cold.

John's busy brain and humour masked a tendency towards melancholy and anxiety. It's a tendency I recognize in myself, a streak in the family psychology that goes back to my grandfather in the hills of West Cork. And soon John's ashes will go there too. Another echo bouncing back.

Gigantic

(What I did on my summer holidays, 1995)

When we arrived in Bremen, Paul was waiting at the airport and he looked very glad to see us. He hugged me tightly and whispered into the nape of my neck, 'I am *very* glad to see you.'

Then he hugged Corncrake, who he barely knew back then, and said, 'Welcome to Bremen.'

In the 1990s, young Irish men did not hug, and it was something Paul had started to do as a way to break away from our repressed programming. I liked it. I hugged everyone I knew when meeting and parting for years, until, many years later, Corncrake said, 'I hate the hugging thing, can we stop the hugging thing?'

People have hidden depths, it turns out, even your best friends. 'OK, Corncrake,' I said, and I started greeting him with a handshake or a fist-bump or a pat on the shoulder.

At Bremen airport in the summer of 1995, however, we were all still hugging. Paul looked tired and a bit dishevelled in the short yellow-orange jacket which he is wearing in almost all of my memories of him.

'Are you still feeling sad?' he said to me. I was. I was feeling quite sad at that time in my life.

Paul carried my rucksack for me for a while, as though we were walking towards a parked car in which he had come to collect us. I took it from him when I realized he had his own rucksack with him, tent and all. (This should have been obvious, but at twenty I wasn't that observant and I was used to people doing things for me.) He had come out to Bremen a week earlier to spend some time by himself before we arrived and he had been camping beneath a bridge beside a disused railway line.

The first night he was there, he said, he heard a rattling roar like nothing he had ever experienced before and realized that it was not a disused railway line at all. A train had passed inches from his head. 'I could have been killed!' he said, and he slapped his leg at how funny this was. This was a thing Paul did – the leg-slapping thing.

On the plus side, he said, there were lots of ripped-up porn magazines under the bridge. We were from a country where porn was basically illegal. It was also an era, for those of you who have grown up with the benefit of the internet, when pornography commonly turned up in bushes and alleyways in this ripped-up form. I've spoken to a lot of people about this since and no one can tell me why it was the case. Were compulsive onanists ripping up porn magazines and dumping them in bushes and alleyways in a post-masturbatory frenzy of shame? Or perhaps this is how porn originally came into being, in snippets of crumpled paper beneath bridges, before being collected, sewn together and ironed by skilled pornographers.

Paul explained, as we walked, that in honour of our arrival in Bremen we would not be staying tonight in his terrifying porn tunnel, but at a family campsite at the edge of town where there were toilets and showers.

'I need a shower,' he added.

'You do,' I agreed.

The campsite was a few miles from the airport, and we walked with our heavy bags. I had brought some hair dye (I planned to dye my hair goth black) and books by Martin Amis and Bret Easton Ellis (it was 1995, a year before I did a course in feminist literature). Paul had brought a large book on massage and some massage oil. Corncrake had brought a little bum bag in which he carried his passport and his money. He also started amassing an 'interesting stones collection' as a self-destructive joke as we heaved our way through the German heat.

We did a lot of walking in the heat that summer, largely because none of us yet knew how to read a bus timetable: we were only twenty years old. It was worse for Corncrake. He spent the summer wearing black woollen jumpers because he believed that sweating was good for the glands.

A few more things about Corncrake, who is my oldest friend.

a) He didn't read novels because he believed that, and I quote, 'Fiction is lies.'

b) He once told me that while he accepted that 'evolution was a fact' ('Very big of you,' I said), he believed Charles Darwin had got things wrong when he said that we had evolved from apes. We had in fact all evolved from different animals. He believed this, he said, because everyone looked like different animals. He came to this belief in honest good faith. He didn't care that Darwin had built his theory on careful observation of the natural world. Corncrake's own theories on the nature of existence were built, like those of the ancient philosophers, on induction and revelation.

c) When we were younger, he had a perfectly shaped quiff like Rick Astley's, while I had an unmanageable cow's lick. I felt terrible envy about his Rick Astley quiff.

'Here we are,' said Paul cheerfully as we panted our way into the entrance of a campsite. We were observed by a large German man with five o'clock shadow across his chin and a dark expression on his forehead.

'Hello, Ulrich!' said Paul. 'These are the friends I told you about.'

Ulrich passed his eyes over me and Corncrake and he shook his head with disappointment, as though Paul had told him that his friends were Arabian princes who would be coming to his cheaply priced German campsite wearing Armani and dripping with gold.

Then he sighed and he told us the rules:

No rubbish.
No staying out late.
Pay upfront.
This is a good, wholesome family campsite. No hanky-panky.

He said all of this in German, except for the word 'hanky-panky' and the sigh. Paul translated the rest for us as we walked to our allotted space between a large blonde family who spent all day sitting on deck chairs watching us and two very attractive German teenagers in a one-man tent who, it turns out, were brother and sister.

'That's a bit weird,' I said.

'Who are we to judge?' said Paul, which made me feel provincial.

We made ourselves at home. As I was a bossy control freak and we were on a tight budget I pooled our money and took control of all the food buying. I went to the local Aldi, where, surrounded by fellow impoverished shoppers – backpackers and homeless people – I was overwhelmed by a Germanic vision of plenty. I bought a week's worth of food in one visit – canned meats, cheeses, soon-to-be rancid coleslaws – oblivious to bourgeois notions like freshness or perishability.

Paul and I, who had the standards of dumpster-diving gutter punks, were happy enough to gorge on our rapidly decomposing food pile, which we kept in the sweltering heat of our tents. Corncrake, being of a more sensitive disposition, was appalled. Apart from anything else, the tents were soon swarming with ants. Over the next few days Corncrake's stomach began to rumble while Paul and I just added ant protein to our diet. Corncrake begged to be able to buy his own groceries. 'I don't want to eat food that's covered with ants,' he said, not unreasonably I can see now, with the benefit of twenty-five years' hindsight.

'Well, food with ants on it is all we have,' I said. 'Take it or leave it!'

This was unfair for many reasons. Corncrake was the

reason we were in Bremen. His father had a mysterious business associate called 'Hans,' who lived there and had promised to source work for him. So Bremen had been Corncrake's choice of summer destination and Paul and I had gone along with it, feeling pretty confident we could source work for ourselves. But 'Hans' proved elusive. Every day, Corncrake attempted to contact him from a payphone in the campsite while Paul and I scoured the city with our CVs.

'"Hans" sounds like a made-up name for a German,' I said to Paul as we lounged around a city centre square. 'Do you think Corncrake is going mad?'

'Possibly,' said Paul, who was studying psychology, before adding, 'Who is to say what "madness" is?'

I can tell you what madness is. One day we came home to find all of our food bags outside of our tents, pinned to improvised wooden spikes. 'To keep the food away from the ants,' Corncrake explained. He understood ant biology about as well as he understood Darwinism. The ants were already climbing up the spikes and into the food. Paul and I just shrugged. Food on spikes was no better or worse than food extracted from a mouldering food pile inside a manky tent.

Ulrich didn't quite see it the same way as we did. He pointed to our Colonel Kurtz-like compound and explained to Paul, in slow, measured German, that we had to go. Rancid meat on wooden spikes was, apparently, 'hanky-panky'. We left the campsite with our bags on our back and our chins in the air, affecting wounded pride. Then we crossed the city to go freeload off some girls from Cork we had met a few days before.

I say we crossed the city but I'm not entirely sure, to be honest, where anything was in Bremen. This is a big short-coming for a memoirist. I'm conscious that this essay roughly fits in with a literary genre that I have, in the past, disparagingly referred to as the 'What I Did on My Summer Holidays' essay. In these essays, writers trace the psychogeography of a beloved European city, often alternating their memories with an account of some local historical or literary figure of note. I cannot do this because I still know absolutely nothing about Bremen.

A few years ago, late at night, my wife and I watched a bit of a German film that was set there. As we watched, parts of the city came into view – a graffitied artistic neighbourhood, a very old building, a nice food market – and each time something new came onscreen my wife would say, 'Do you remember that from Bremen?'

And each time I'd shake my head and say: 'No . . .' or, when I was embarrassed, 'Maybe?'

'Were you in Bremen at all?' said my wife eventually.

'I think so,' I said, though I was beginning to feel unsure. Occasionally I'm tempted to Google 'Bremen' to see what I recognize, but I can't get broadband out in my writing shed. Yes, even now my lack of intellectual curiosity about the city is shocking.

As for the biographical details of some erstwhile Bremen citizen of note that I might weave through this narrative to give it some intellectual heft, I'm also at a loss. There are the Musicians of Bremen, I suppose, those stars of nursery-rhyme and farm. But I don't think they kept diaries, what with being a donkey, a dog, a cat and a hen. And their main achievement seems to be climbing on top of each other and braying at people.

We first met the Cork girls while we were lying around in the heat of a park that I didn't catch the name of, in a city I'm pretty sure was Bremen. As we lazed, Paul noticed three pretty girls walking by who looked a little paler and more confused than everyone else, and he assumed, correctly, that they were Irish. He climbed over the fence to talk to them.

Paul was like a human sociology experiment at this point in his life. When I first met him, he had been a shy first-year who had just transferred from a business course in another college, and I was an assured second-year Arts pseud. Two years later, studying psychology had caused him to lose his inhibitions at just around the same time I was having a bout of existential despair. So our roles reversed. Going up to introduce himself to strange women was exactly the sort of thing Paul was good at, at this point in his life. (In fact, I met the woman who became my wife because Paul started chatting to her friend in the college library.) I'd watch him in action with a certain amount of detached awe. 'Marvellous,' I would say to myself from time to time while watching Paul.

A few more things about Paul:

a) He dressed like a dandy hobo, a mix of dapper thrift-store suits and random stabs of insane anti-fashion gestures (rat's tails, bobble hats, tracksuit bottoms).

b) He listened to both eighties hair metal and anarchist punk bands. He had developed a sort of scavenger mentality, which resulted in us regularly eating food found at the side of the road and, on one occasion, sitting down to finish an abandoned meal on the street-side table of a fancy restaurant.

c) He had a priestly disposition that led to people pouring their heart out to him. This I did daily.

d) He was a great dancer.

The Cork girls were funny arty sorts and they were just as lonely and lost as we were. They arranged to meet us later in an Irish bar that we hadn't known existed. We decided to celebrate by drinking German beer in the park. When we arrived at the bar that night Corncrake and I went straight to the bathroom while Paul made conversation. Unfortunately, Corncrake had trouble distinguishing his trouser zip from that of his bumbag and proceeded to wet himself at the urinal. He spent the rest of the night blowdrying his crotch with a hand-dryer while I checked on him sporadically.

'It's been a good excuse to practise my German,' he said stoically, before initiating a conversation with a urinating stranger in oddly accented English.

'I haf whet my throus-airs und am thrying it with theez breeze-machone,' he said, his crotch pressed to a wheezing blast of hot air.

'I don't think that's German,' I said, and he looked at me, perplexed and drunk. I was perplexed and drunk too. So maybe it *was* German. Who knows? I wasn't good at German either.

I hung out with Corncrake in the toilets for a while. Outside, Paul was laying the groundwork for the annexation of the Cork girls' flat a few days later. It wasn't part of some great masterplan. We were not sophisticated gigolo grifters moving from town to town on the money of easily befuddled rich ladies. We weren't that organized. What we were, and what the Cork girls were not prepared for, was an unholy mix of helpless and entitled. They lived in recommissioned student accommodation alongside several international students. After Ulrich evicted us, we moved into their sitting room with our mouldering groceries and rotting clothes and began to eat all of their food. I think we could have contentedly spent the summer there. But when one of their flatmates complained about us – we'd eaten a stew he'd been saving, because we were pigs – we were asked to leave.

That's when we moved to some wasteland on the university grounds, pitching our tents discreetly amid some bushes. In a way, that's where we became the truest reflection of who we really were. We would laze about in the sun, going sporadically to use the showers in the university gym. I remember coming back one day to find Paul standing naked and reading a book outside his tent.

'My clothes are dirty,' he explained.

'Why don't you wash them?'

'They'll just get dirty again.'

'We really need to get jobs,' I said, sensing that we were going to the dogs. I don't know how I knew we were going to the dogs. I just did. I struggle to recall how my brain functioned back then.

What did I want from life? It's hard to remember now.

a) I had no real ambition to speak of. At least, not in a conventional sense.

b) I wanted to be part of something called the 'counterculture' that involved weird post-punk music and underground publishing and vaguely sketched-out 'creative' lifestyles. I wanted to meet cool German girls with dyed hair and to live in a squat and to be better at guitar than I was. I wanted something to happen.

c) I wanted to be happy. I had recently had an intuition that the universe was empty and meaningless and that I was empty and meaningless. I got on with things, because that's what I do, but this feeling was proving hard to shake.

d) And in the short term I wanted a job washing dishes so I didn't have to go home.

In the end, I became so motivated that I found two jobs. The first was in the kitchen of a Chinese restaurant. But this didn't pay enough money to live on, so I got a second job in a fancy restaurant on a fancy square. I got this one thanks to a glassy-eyed, flatly spoken American manager. His hair was the same beige colour as his face and his slacks. He worked surrounded by Germans and Turks and he seemed eager to speak English with someone.

'Where are you from?' he asked.

'Ireland.'

'Ah,' he said. 'Trying to escape the war.'

'The war?' I said, before remembering the only stuff about Ireland that made the international news in 1995. 'Oh yes, the war. It doesn't really affect us down in Dublin.'

He looked at me with sad eyes. He clutched my shoulder and squeezed it, apparently impressed by my stoicism and bravery. 'We don't have to talk about it if you don't want to,' he said.

'It has been hard for me,' I said, after a very uncomfortable silence.

'I've lost people too,' he said, which made me feel guilty because I hadn't really lost anyone then and this man surely had some very tragic backstory to lead him here to one of Germany's least acclaimed cities. He gave me the job.

Now I had two jobs, so I gifted the lower-paid one to Paul and I started to focus on my new career. My new career involved arriving to the restaurant at six in the morning, when I would drink approximately four pints of free Coke and begin mopping the floors (badly) and washing the previous night's dishes (badly).

My main colleague was an elderly woman who fed me watermelon and, in a language I didn't recognize, chastised me good-humouredly for my shoddy washing-up skills. She refused to believe that I didn't understand her. The American manager would sometimes come in and sit down beside me to make conversation that dwindled to nothing before he eventually looked uncomfortable, got up and left.

At the time I thought, 'Thank God,' whenever he left.

Now I think, 'Poor lonely, boring man. I should have made more of an effort.'

In the evenings, Paul and I took to hanging around in the local park and sometimes, if we missed the bus to the waste-land where we lived, we'd sleep there. One night we met a good-looking Turkish boy in a crop top and embroidered jeans, and sometimes he'd sit with us and share a joint. We'd talk about Paul's search for a better job and he'd talk about Turkey and how much he missed it. He had very good English and a lopsided smile that would quickly change into a lopsided frown.

Once he said, looking us up and down as he did so, that there was a lot of work to be had late at night down at the docks. Then he shrugged. 'Well, I'd better get back to work,' he said, and walked off into the gloom of the park.

'We should go see about that work down the docks,' said Paul.

The next night at around midnight, Corncrake, who was still trying to get in touch with Hans, was already in his sleeping bag when I shook him awake. 'Get up and go down the docks with Paul,' I said.

'I don't want to go down the docks with Paul,' said Corncrake. 'Why do I have to go down the docks?'

'Because a guy we met in the park told us there was work there,' said Paul.

'Who is this guy?' said Corncrake.

'We meet him in the park when we sleep there,' said Paul.

'Why is he in a park *at night*?' said Corncrake.

'He works there,' said Paul. 'He's cool.'

'He shares a joint with us sometimes,' I said.

'He's cool,' said Paul. 'He wears a crop-top and embroidered jeans.'

'He sounds like he's a rent boy,' said Corncrake.

Hearing Corncrake say it, I had to accept that he did sound like a rent boy. I had suspected this. In retrospect, I am 100 per cent sure he was a rent boy. But I also really, really didn't want to be left alone in Germany and, if that meant pimping my best friends out to dock folk, I was apparently OK with that. Like I said, I can't entirely remember my motivations at this time in my life.

'He's not a rent boy,' said Paul. 'He works for the parks department.'

I looked at Paul. Paul was, in many ways, a very sophisticated man, but he really did believe this. In his view, it was plausible that a joint-smoking hottie in a crop top did mysterious work for the Bremen parks department late at night.

'Yeah, Corncrake,' I said. 'He works for the parks department. Now get up and go down the docks with Paul.'

'I don't want to go down the docks,' said Corncrake, in the same tone of voice in which he had previously said, 'I don't want to eat food covered in ants.' He was hard work.

Paul went down the docks alone and couldn't see where any work was to be found. This was presumably because he thought that it had something to do with loading boats, not turning tricks for sailors. I should really have gone there with him.

Funnily enough, it was the next day that 'Hans' came through and Corncrake was offered a job in a branch of

McDonald's. He just had to undergo a medical first, a normal, regular procedure. 'Just something we do here in Germany,' said Hans.

'Well, well, so apparently, "Hans" does exist,' I said.

'I know, right?' said Paul.

Corncrake decided to ring his family with the good news, but he only did so after we'd done a lot of 'celebrating'. By this time, he had completely forgotten the word 'medical' and I know this because I heard one side of the conversation from outside the phone box.

'So, I start on Tuesday,' said Corncrake into the receiver, 'but first I have to have an operation.'

'An operation,' said Corncrake.

'An operation,' said Corncrake. 'So I can work in McDonald's.'

'An operation,' said Corncrake. 'Just something they do here in Germany.'

'So. I. Can. Work. In. McDonald's,' said Corncrake. 'It's just an operation.'

'An operation. That's just something they do here in Germany,' said Corncrake.

'An operation,' said Corncrake.

'Yes, an operation because before you start work you have to have an operation,' said Corncrake. 'After the operation I can start the job.'

'An operation,' said Corncrake. 'To work in McDonald's.'

'*That's just what they do here,*' said Corncrake. '*An operation. Then I can work in McDonald's.*'

'Oh my God,' said Corncrake after he hung up. 'My

parents don't understand why I have to have an operation to work in McDonald's.'

I rang home. 'Does Corncrake have to have an operation in order to work in McDonald's?' asked my mother.

'Probably,' I said. 'What have you heard?'

Around this time, Corncrake and I, now wage earners, decided to forego the life we had made for ourselves in the waste ground near the university to move to an attic room in an even further-flung suburb. Our new landlady, Martina, was an attractive middle-aged woman with dyed red hair and, initially, she seemed thrilled to have us there. She showed us an old-fashioned biscuit tin, filled with pills, tabs, strange vials and a big block of hash.

'This is my box of drugs,' she said.

'Yes, of course,' I said, in case reacting otherwise to a box of drugs was considered gauche.

'I get them when I go to Amsterdam,' she said.

'Ah yes, Amsterdam,' I said, hoping she thought I went there often.

Then she passed her manicured fingernails over the drugs box magnanimously. 'Take what you like.'

'What are the pills?' asked Paul.

Martina shrugged. 'I don't know. Do you want one?'

'You're fine, thanks,' said Paul.

'Maybe I'll have some of the hash,' I said, and four hours later I was crouched in a paranoid heap in the corner of Martina's kitchen telling Corncrake to stop laughing at me.

'Sure, I'll try the poppers while you have it open,' I said

on another night. I did. It was like a headache in a bottle. I tried it again. It was still like a headache in a bottle. So I tried it again just in case. And again.

Paul was still more or less jobless, but he eventually found a room of his own in one of the student flats near where the Cork girls lived. They were still very nice to us, God love them. Paul shared his flat with a smattering of slightly older international stoners who collected erotic comic books and made huge vegetarian stews and treated us like pets. They took us to a Babes in Toyland gig and, one moon-bright night, they fed us hash brownies until Paul and I hallucinated a gnome and followed him around the Bremen suburbs.

'I don't think he's real,' I said after a few hours.

'Shhh, he'll *hear* you,' said Paul.

We settled into a low-wage, high-squalor routine for the summer. Corncrake wrote, 'Interesting stones collection' on a bit of card and put his now excessively large collection of rocks on a little side table in our bedroom. There was a television on which we endlessly watched the OJ trial and MTV Europe. It got very hot in our attic, but we never once changed our sheets. Paul, who spent half his time in our flat, practised massage techniques on us. He and I bought Spanish guitars in a flea market and began trying to write songs for the band we had started with our friend D. But we mainly played Pixies songs. I particularly liked 'Gigantic' and I'd sing it for Paul before we went out on a caper. (He's kind of namechecked in it.)

Having discovered the flea market, we also bought second-hand leather jackets, replica medieval weaponry and old rusty bikes. Mine had a flaw that meant the pedal would stall and jerk my knee painfully with every revolution. One morning as I cycled to work on this bike in the warm dawn sunlight, I realized that, for the first time in a long time, I wasn't sad. I was happy.

About a month before, early on in our time in Bremen, we decided to go for a walk down to a lake that the Cork girls had told us about. German teenagers and students were gathered in little groups around the shore drinking, playing guitar and tending campfires.

'Let's go for a swim,' said Paul, and as this fitted my self-image as a devil-may-care rulebreaker we stripped off all of our clothes and strode in.

'Look at us go,' I thought. 'We just don't give a shit. *In your face*, bourgeois society.'

We splashed around delightfully for a while until I realized three things:

It was freezing.
Corncrake was not with us.
Our clothes were no longer where we had left them
    on the bank.

We called Corncrake's name. Then shouted his name. Then screamed his name.

'We'll have to get out of the water,' said Paul. 'Or we'll die of hypothermia.'

Across from us, past a little bit of beach where our clothes had been, there were some bushes. We ran across the sand

and lay down in them for a while, screaming Corncrake's name.

On the other side of the bushes there was a path that led back to the suburbs. Young Germans cycled by. We lay there, trying to look casual – just two naked dudes screaming in a bush. When they made eye contact I shrugged as if to say, 'Hey, what are you gonna do? We're hanging out naked in a bush, *get over it.*'

After a while we decided that Corncrake was not coming back, nor were our clothes, and we would have to start nudely making our way home. It was getting dark now. We ran along the narrow roadway, jumping into a ditch whenever we saw the lights of bikes, or, at one point, a police car. I remember lying in the ditch for a while, looking at Paul, who was resting his eyes.

'Maybe we should wait until morning,' I said.

'OK,' said Paul. Then his eyes opened. 'It will be bright in the morning,' he said, which was very true.

We began running again. We got into a bit of a rhythm. At one point we ran through a field that turned out to be filled with nettles. We were, miraculously, not stung and this emboldened us. At another junction we had to crouch in some undergrowth before deciding we had no option but to race past a beer garden full of drinking Germans. They cheered us on.

Then we were on the home stretch – running alongside a stream less than half a mile from our tents. We had reached a cluster of apartment buildings when I saw Corncrake in the distance.

He ran up to us, a little out of breath because, I suppose, he had the extra weight of clothes to contend with.

'Oh, thank God,' he said. 'I thought you'd drowned.' Then he looked at us and fell over laughing.

An hour or so previously, Corncrake had, on seeing us in the water, figured it would be very funny to hide our clothes. Then he thought it would be even funnier to get a photograph of us naked. So, with his inept German he went around asking the nearby teenagers if he could borrow a camera in order to capture our nudity on film. This was, in case you've forgotten, an era when camera film had to be sent away to be developed.

'What did you think they'd do?' I asked. 'Get your weird homoerotic glamour shots developed and then post them to you?'

'Oh,' he said. 'I hadn't thought about that.'

His search for a camera took so long that when Corncrake came back to where we had been swimming, we were gone. He instantly worried that we'd drowned, that he'd killed us.

'And then you thought, "I'm going to miss my good friends Paul and Patrick and now I am alone in Germany with really shit German,"' said Paul.

'I thought, "I'm going to be in so much trouble with my parents."'

'Where are our clothes?' I asked.

'I don't know,' he said. 'I hid them somewhere and now I can't find them.'

I'm not normally a violent man but I kicked him so hard on the arse that I worried I'd broken a bone in my foot.

Corncrake gave Paul his T-shirt and gave me his woollen jumper and then he limped away to try and find our clothes. Corncrake was shorter than Paul and I, so it now looked like we were wearing weird belly tops. We were also still naked from the waist down, a look usually favoured by cartoon animals and middle-aged swingers on late-night sex documentaries. I looked up and saw several people on the balconies gazing down at us. It was only around half past ten in the evening. An older woman waved. Paul waved back. We walked home.

Several years later, I heard Paul tell the story of our naked run to some friends at a party. He told it a little differently than I just have. He skirted over the embarrassment and the anger and the balcony voyeurs. He talked about the wind in our lungs and on our skin and the sweet smell of the trees and the strange lack of inhibitions he felt running naked alongside his friend in the German suburbs. And for a moment I remembered it that way too.

The Golden Age of Piracy

In the hazy autumn of 1995, I returned to Dublin with Paul and Corncrake to find that our friend D was in the process of taking over an anarcho-syndicalist pirate-radio station. D was, by then, the boss of me and all of our friends and this meant that soon most of us were helping to run an anarcho-syndicalist pirate-radio station. I mean, what else would we be doing with ourselves?

I was not surprised that D was in the process of acquiring an anarcho-syndicalist pirate-radio station because D had a way of stepping into things when they were on their last legs and slowly taking them over. I believe in Trotskyist circles this is known as 'entryism', but at that point I wouldn't have known that because I hadn't actually read Trotsky (though I'd pretended I had). D's takeovers were never entirely pre-meditated. It's just that D is a confident man of action.

He had done something similar with the college Video Society. I can remember only two committee members who weren't friends of D's. There was a wily young Kerryman and a ridiculously handsome English boy named Tristram who wore a cowboy hat and lived in a hotel. In those days a name like Tristram was rare enough in Ireland. He might as well have been called Gandalf or Aslan.

'My aunt has bought a village in Sicily which she is turning into an artists' colony, and I'm going to go down and help her for the summer,' he told me once.

'I'm going to work in a kebab shop,' I said, which hopefully sounded just as exotic to him.

We didn't quite usher in a second golden age of cinema at the Video Society. However, the parties were good and we made a few short films that I never figured out how to get off the archaic editing machine, and when the treasurer ran off with all of the money we managed to get it back by snitching to his parents.

I don't know how snitching fits into anarcho-syndicalism, but it certainly fits into the Soviet understanding of Marxism, so I was happy enough with this outcome. Then I became treasurer, which led to me having a huge panic attack while staring at a ledger. D ended up having to do the accounts all by himself.

And that right there is why he always ended up running things.

The anarcho-syndicalist pirate-radio station had been around for some time. There had been a pirate-radio boom in Ireland in the 1980s, largely because there was no legal alternative to the state broadcaster, RTÉ. Some people made a lot of money from it. Our station rode the tail end of that boom in the way only an anarchist organization uninterested in money can ride a boom, by building up a cool reputation for itself among broke punks and radicals and pseuds. In the autumn of 1995, however, it was at a low ebb. Its notable surviving DJs included a pleasantly Eeyorish chap named Dano who sold cassettes on O'Connell Bridge and had excellent musical taste. He also had excellent weed. We turned on the radio one night to find him broadcasting the sound of his own snoring across the North inner city. It was far from the worst thing we broadcast.

There was also a man called Pondlife Pete who had bleached hair, came to meetings flanked by his two girlfriends and apparently used his show as a platform for a lucrative drug-dealing business. He sent out coded messages to his customer base about where he would be and what he would be selling. He played terrible street punk as a sort of afterthought.

Then there was Aidan Walsh, a true-blue Dublin city eccentric with a frizz of long black hair tamed by a trucker hat. In those days he took photos at every minor Dublin gig and his home was said to be filled with unprocessed film. At our meetings he'd constantly ask about getting more exposure for his programme, under the impression that we had a marketing budget. He would start his sentences with the words, 'As a celebrity . . .'

To be fair, he was a sort of celebrity. In the eighties he had been friends with the avant-garde post-punk friends-of-Bono the Virgin Prunes, and he had a couple of novelty hits, including 'The Community Games', which included the words: 'I like throwing the bow and arrow at the community games.'

As a pirate-radio colleague, he was a bit of a liability. He would regularly invite strangers into the studio, leaving them with the run of the house. D once went over to the local shop while Aidan was meant to be on the air. Aidan was there buying milk for tea while the stranger he was interviewing held forth live on the radio. 'Now what you have to remember about the "so-called moon landing" is . . .'

D's introduction to the station came from his friend M, who was simultaneously an accountant and an Ecstasy-gobbling dance fiend. There was S, an American vegan, who lived in the slightly mouldy red-brick terraced house from which the station broadcast. He and the other vegans connected to the station spent much of their spare time preparing beans for vegan stews. And there was another anarcho-punk named Derek, who was, or at least *seemed*, slightly older and had bookshelves made of concrete blocks and planks, fully stocked with graphic novels and underground publications, with which I was very impressed. This looked like an excellent model for adulthood to me at the time (and still does).

Together they gave the station a new name and set out to reorganize and rebrand it. They printed up T-shirts, vastly overestimating demand. I slept in those T-shirts for years. (As an aside, for a long time I didn't understand why anyone needed to buy T-shirts. Whenever I see someone buying a T-shirt my brain always thinks, 'Surely you have several large cardboard boxes in your attic filled with the T-shirts you over-optimistically created for your pirate-radio station and/or band?' I have a lifetime's supply of T-shirts. As I have aged, however, I have learned that some people did not mass-produce unsaleable merchandise at an earlier point in their lives. Some people need to buy T-shirts from a shop.)

D imported his bandmates, his flatmates and his friends to fill in gaps in the roster. There were some serious music aficionados in our midst, who had wonderful taste in techno or American hardcore or folk and were happy to share this with the few square miles of broadcast coverage our radio station could manage.

My then-girlfriend, Diana, and our friend Claire had a brilliant show broadcasting the weirder bits of vinyl they found in charity shops – obscure novelty acts, exploitation genre music, weirder country 'n' Irish performers and Jane Fonda workout albums. They didn't take things too seriously. Their DJ names were I Choose to Trust in God and DJ Lada. There were also a few shows that, I seem to recall, involved the reading aloud of political tracts. I had a show with another friend, Paul P (I know this is confusing, but around 50 per cent of Irish males in my generation seem to be called Paul). This was styled as satirical but was hampered by the fact we had very different ideas about what satire was. Paul P preferred his work to be off-the-cuff. He liked to, as he put it, 'rant'. This was a period in Earth history when every group of counterculturally inclined young people had one friend who did 'rants' whenever he had a few beers in him. Usually these rants were about 'the Man' and they were satirical and conspiratorially minded. This really was a thing in the 1990s. It was something we did before young men with too much time on their hands discovered 'going to therapy' and 'internet trolling'. I thought his rants were very funny and felt that we were serving the nation by putting them on the air.

My contribution to the show was self-penned surrealist comedy sketches. Having no access to actors, I read these aloud, doing all the voices myself. I did so in the flat tone of a depressed newsreader or an uninspired priest. A flatmate tuned in once and said: 'It was funny for a couple of minutes and then it was confusing and then it was depressing. Why are you doing this?'

Why indeed? Why do any of us do what we do? 'Why are you doing this?' was a question I heard a lot in my early twenties.

At the core of our pirate-radio station was 'politics'. This was the countercultural anarchism and Marxism that we informed ourselves about through American and British 'zines and punk records. Bob Dylan writes in *Chronicles* that for a while 'news' for him was the stories of fires and fights and miscarriages of justice he heard in early-twentieth-century folk songs. For me, 'news' was largely whatever punk stalwarts like Jello Biafra or Steve Ignorant had sung about ten years before. And so, in 1995 we were right up to date on current issues for young people in Ireland, like what Thatcher was doing to the miners and what Tipper Gore was doing to censor hip-hop in the 1980s. I never read an Irish newspaper. I think I knew who the Taoiseach was in 1995, but please don't test me.

The most important message we imbibed from US and UK punk, however, was that we could do things for ourselves. We could make culture and art and broadcast and distribute it. Our transmitter was a bit ropey, but we made do. We bounced our signal from one transmitter in a studio in the mouldy terraced house in North Dublin to another on the roof of a city-centre café called the Garden of Delight run by another anarchist collective (in those days, you couldn't throw a rock in Dublin without hitting an anarchist collective). I remember sticking an aerial up there with D one windy day and both of us suddenly becoming gripped with an Orwellian fear that we were being filmed by pirate-radio-obsessed stooges of the establishment. Nowadays, of course, we would probably livestream it all ourselves.

We produced leaflets that we cut and pasted together and filled with reviews and news. A fan of in-jokes, I compared every band I wrote about to slacker lo-fi stalwarts Pavement, even when the comparison was completely inaccurate. I thought this was hilarious. The photocopying section of Reads stationery shop on Nassau Street was our office and I developed an almost erotic love for good stationery – hardback diaries, nice ballpoint pens.

We also held fundraising events at the Garden of Delight, typically open-mic nights. I would hustle people to come and perform, and I'd design posters and flyers and assemble 'anarcho-syndicalist goodie bags' featuring self-satirizing slo-gans and pacifist toy soldiers (I cut their guns off) and sweets. The food at the café was usually vegan, but I'd often sneak across to Beshoffs takeaway to get a burger. I aspired to be vegan in the same way St Augustine aspired to be chaste.

Our address was listed in punk 'zines, and we attracted free records from labels all over the world and received visits from attractive international anarchists. 'Why are you *here*?' I'd wonder of these exotic weirdos. There was a beautiful French girl with purple hair, and there was a Belgian guy who looked like River Phoenix and who a female friend said it actually hurt to look at. These hot foreigners caused romantic chaos in our ranks. There were love triangles and love squares and love dodecahedrons. It wasn't our fault. I think it was just the first time any of us had seen cheekbones.

Our organizational meetings were held upstairs in a nearby pub. A lot of the meetings were spent discussing how to further the cause of far-left politics. I remember men in parkas giddily talking over the only women in the room in order to make interesting points about feminism. I remember one soul-rending discussion about how we needed to involve more people of colour in the station. I left worried that some of the more committed anarchists were about to go out and kidnap people to make up numbers.

The anarcho-syndicalists who had stuck around were under the impression that they were an autonomous collective with no centralized leadership. They were obsessed with 'consensus'. I had never seen 'consensus' as a bad word before this time in my life, but that was to change. These people liked to take a vote on *everything*. You could only ever get anything done when everyone agreed to the exact course of action, which meant it was ridiculously difficult to get anything done. So, as happens in collectives, communication got wilfully bad in the station. Conversations like this would happen:

'I see you fixed the broken window. When did we agree to do that?'

'What? You didn't hear about the meeting? Oh, that's terrible! You could have intervened! And now we've gone ahead and fixed the window rather than form a "window-fixing steering committee" like you suggested.'

'Yes, but now we need to break the window again and form a "window-fixing steering committee".'

After five minutes in an anarchist collective I began to crave centralized government. I began describing myself as a Marxist. I hadn't read any Marx, just like I hadn't read any Trotsky, but I didn't feel like I had to, because no one else I knew had read Marx either and I knew loads of Marxist-sounding words like 'capitalist' and 'bourgeois'. I particularly loved the sound of Marx's 'dictatorship of the proletariat' and began evoking it all the time, even though I didn't really know what it meant. I just assumed that *I* was the 'proletariat' of whom Marx wrote.

For the record, I did go on to read the *Communist Manifesto* a few years later. In a remainder bookshop I picked up a special 'deluxe edition' – which doesn't feel quite in the spirit of what Marx was trying to achieve. In fact, it feels a little like the publishers were deliberately trolling him. I liked the *Communist Manifesto*. You know what? I think Karl Marx might have been on to something.

OK, we meant well. While we were a bit naïve, the station was, for a lot of us, a gateway into genuine politicization. It was our first time thinking about power and representation and it came from a real desire to be engaged with the world. Several of the things we went on and on about which were considered radical in 1996 – gay marriage, abortion rights, sex positivity – have become mainstream notions now. I even got my first pragmatic insight into male privilege after one of our meetings when Diana said, 'You know, you guys talk an *awful* lot. It would be great if you let us get a word in edgeways.' I realized that I did talk a lot and that it might be a good idea to shut up more.

A lot of our meetings were actually spent talking about how the Man wanted to shut us down because of our insurrectionary ideas. We assumed that there was a squad in Pearse Street Garda station dedicated to ending the likes of us. Consequently, time that probably should have been spent on our programming was spent putting together sophisticated security-camera systems and a zipline that would allow us to detach our illegal transmitter and jettison it into a neighbour's garden in case of a police raid. There were lots of rumours about police raids in those days. We regularly ran drills in which we sent the transmitter down the zipline while someone clutched a stopwatch.

This sense of urgency didn't, of course, stop stoned DJs or Aidan Walsh or me forgetting to shut the front door, but I very much enjoyed all of the cloak-and-dagger stuff and I spent a lot of time on rooftops feeling transgressive. We definitely spent a bit too much time on rooftops, when I think about it now.

We moved on from the station after a while and other people took over. Those people presumably think *their* era was the golden age of that station, the fools. In recent years some people started operating again under the station's original name. This iteration is, of course, online, where it is completely legal to broadcast but where it is no less politically important to speak your mind. I love that people can publish and broadcast so easily now, but I still have a bit of a yen for the days when publishing involved glue and photocopiers and when broadcasting involved highfalutin sociological notions and hanging out on rooftops and breaking the law.

One of my most vivid/terrifying memories, when I think about it now, is of watching a fellow DJ plummet past the studio window after he went up to adjust an aerial.

'I'm fine,' he said, as he lay among some scattered beer kegs in the back yard, and I took his word for it. Taking him to an institution as organized as a 'hospital' would have been too much of a concession to the Man, I guess. Or, possibly, we didn't go to the hospital because the boy was American and maybe he was concussed and he forgot that the hospitals in Ireland were more or less free if you turned up having fallen off a roof. Given how much American punk we listened to in that radio station, I probably didn't know that the hospitals were free either.

We only realized that all of this drilling and ziplining and plummeting from roofs was a terrible waste of our time when one day we got a very polite phone call from the Man (or a garda representing Him) asking would we mind turning our transmitter off for a while as it was interfering with local emergency-radio signals.

'How did you get this number?' we asked.

'Oh, don't you worry about that,' said the Man. He sounded nice, to be honest.

Subsequently, a friend at a bigger pirate radio station told us what actually happened if the guards came and took your transmitter: you called around and collected it from the police station the next day. 'They're usually very good about it,' he said.

How to Make Music and
Influence Nobody

In 2007 my friend Paul connected with me on Facebook. In the 'how you know each other' section, he wrote 'shared a rich fantasy life for many years'.

What he meant was that we'd been in a band together. Our friend D was in the band as well: it was a *folie à trois*. We called ourselves the National Prayer Breakfast, after a political event in the US of which we had little understanding. After a while the name was abbreviated to the NPB because people kept mishearing it when we rang them looking for gigs. 'The Nashville Perv Basket?' said one booker. 'The Nautical Perp Biscuits?' said another.

Around this time we were also running a pirate-radio station. We didn't really know how to run a pirate-radio station. We didn't really know how to be in a band, either. We could barely play. At our early practices Paul used a suitcase as his bass drum. I knew how to play in one time signature, D another. We glugged down instant coffee in a Parnell Street rehearsal studio as we all sang, rasped or yelped and put distortion on everything. We were very loud and our ears rang all the time.

We loved the *idea* of being in a band. We created our own little world. We designed weird posters and put them up around town before we ever had gigs. We didn't realize that you couldn't just slap posters on city lamp-posts until we received some expensive littering fines in the post. (If we had realized this, we probably wouldn't have put our address on the posters.)

Paul and I scoured charity shops for suitable stage clothes (a brown velvet suit? Marching-band jackets?). We bought a Casio keyboard for a hundred pounds and used it on everything (the best setting was 'vibraphone', which we used on our politically confused song 'Gun Control'). We had stage names – Kinky, Bim Bim and Donut at first; then later, Wayne Freyne, Lance Clancy and Jobey-Joe Keogh. We wrote fantastical stories about these fictionalized versions of ourselves and included them in fake newspapers we made and gave out at gigs. We put on strange posh/American/ British accents in early interviews. I have no idea why. I found a recording of an old pirate-radio interview recently and my accent is from nowhere I can place.

We were inspired by everything. We read a lot and randomly rhymed things we barely understood for lyrics ('I'll swap your aesthetics for morphogenetics!' I sang on a song called 'The Karl Marx Experience'). We named songs after people we liked: 'Gustav Klimt', 'Manu Chao', 'Kim Novak' and 'Schubert Shebop'. None of these were about the people they were named after. We produced 'hymn books' filled with lyrics and illustrated with strange cartoons I drew, and we distributed them at gigs.

We sent our weird early tapes and bizarre pamphlets to celebrities and music critics we liked. I once got a confused phone call from veteran scenester BP Fallon. 'Why did you send me this?' he asked. I said, accurately, that I didn't know.

We put on all-ages daytime gigs in underused ballrooms like the Ierne Ballroom, which had wood-panelled walls and a glitter ball hanging from the ceiling, and now-defunct venues like the Funnel. The Funnel was down in the docklands. Outside in the financial centre, a new breed of aspirational, besuited young Dubliner was wandering around mastering the universe, but we didn't notice, busy as we were distributing free sweets and melted ice-cream and encouraging people to play the board games that a light-fingered friend had liberated from a nearby toy shop.

We jumped around a lot on stage, which sort of made up for the fact we weren't playing particularly well. We played with bands like Das Madman (who became the Jimmy Cake), Bobby Pulls a Wilson and Palomine (the latter containing future members of The Chalets and the Connect Four Orchestra). Those bands tended to get good reviews from the 'zines that covered such things. We did not. 'I don't get it,' said one unimpressed reviewer. At this point we were, unknown to ourselves, outsider artists. I had a handlebar moustache (this was fifteen years before hipsters reclaimed moustaches). Paul had grown a luxuriant rat's tail. D sometimes wore his hair in little bunches.

We became obsessed with being excluded from 'the scene', but in reality we always had an extended family of creative friends helping us, and a cadre of fellow musicians who played with the band for spells of time. Around this time, the large pirate-radio station Phantom FM latched on to one of our songs, 'Feeding Frenzy', thanks largely, I think, to me yelling the words 'Pirate station!' at regular intervals. We made a video for 'Feeding Frenzy' in which we pretended to hold up a late-night petrol station where Paul worked. The real police were called. 'Be more careful with your "art",' said the sergeant angrily. Loads of youngsters started coming to the gigs.

One day we got a phone call from a schoolboy called James Byrne. He had heard our band on Phantom and couldn't believe he was talking to us. His band, Deputy Fuzz, were recording an album on an eight-track recorder. We put it out on our label, Catchy Go Go Records. We started putting out the music of other artists: 46 Long, Herm, Adrian Crowley. Our headquarters was a house in Josephine Avenue that D and I shared and in which he continued to live until very recently. We were on the dole. We aspired to be like Motown and we got our address listed in all of the international music directories. People sent *us* tapes. Once, we were visited by two Norwegian musicians who were perplexed to discover Catchy Go Go Records was just some scruffy young men in a red-brick terraced house in North Dublin.

We worked hard, harder than our friends who had real jobs. We wanted to create and to be successful and to mean something. Being part of a band is all about wanting, really. So we had big, theatrical fights about what we wanted and what we stood for. Once, we argued into the night about whether we would accept money from Guinness to do an ad ('It would be politically wrong.' 'But it would be a lot of

money.' 'They're a corporation!' 'But we drink Guinness.').
Incidentally, Guinness had not offered us money to do an ad.
Guinness never offered us money to do an ad. We just
thought it was an important principle that needed to be
argued about.

We churned out hundreds of songs, losing ourselves in
eight-track overdubs in a big garage in Paul's family home in
Foxrock. We made punk songs and swing songs and country
songs and hip-hop songs. We'd take breaks to eat all the
food in the family fridge while simultaneously pontificating
about badly understood far-left politics. Paul's lovely dad
advised us to start pensions and to think about the future.
He was clearly worried; he'd inherited two new adult
mouths to feed for several days every week. If only he knew.
We did think about the future, but in it we were politically
correct DIY millionaires – like Fugazi, only rich – possibly
solving crime in our spare time. I never started a pension.

Still, we had more bureaucracy than the civil service.
Our world was filled with charts and plans. We took minutes at our daily band meetings. We would censure newly
conscripted band members for breaking step sartorially
('Was that an appropriate shirt choice, Jeremy?' we'd say, in
what amounted to a show trial). D had a huge hardback
ledger with impressive-looking to-do lists and financial cal-
culations. He would convince us to go on tours of Ireland
and the UK. We toured Britain five times, despite having no
money. He took to wearing a cowboy hat like JR Ewing in
Dallas.

We slept on couches and travelled in two vehicles:

a hatchback and a decommissioned hearse that had been illegally made to look like a police car (there was a siren and everything). Our driver, Ian, didn't have an operational driving licence, but he did have a bowler hat, a pleasant demeanour and a way with customs officials.

Being on tour with your friends is like running away with the circus. And, like running away with the circus, I thoroughly recommend it. We played to five people in Cardiff, three people in Manchester and a full house in Camden's Dublin Castle. We asked for directions at the 'highest pub in Wales'. We watched the sun set over cornfields from a trailer in Oxford. In a moonlit bay in Cornwall we swam in a phosphorescent sea. We sang karaoke with a Roy Orbison lookalike in Penryn. We marvelled at Britain's many motorway service stations. In Camden Town D and Paul spent the entire tour budget on designer trousers that looked like chaps. 'They go with the cowboy hat,' explained Paul. In revenge, I spent a similar amount of money on an impractical tailor-made white suit. Several tours later, this heavily stained item could walk from the car to the venue all by itself.

We got good reviews and worked with a big producer called Gordon Raphael, but we were once told by our English manager that we weren't rock 'n' roll enough. That night one of us got drunk and threw a bottle across a crowded backstage area at a gig by Soundtrack of our Lives. The next night our guitarist was ejected from the Hives' aftershow party and was chased by security guards through Hyde Park. But our experiments with rock 'n' roll behaviour stopped there. There are no 'my drug hells' in this story. Being in a band is intense enough without chemical interference.

People usually form their first bands at the same time that they're detaching from their family. A band is basically a surrogate family and, like a family, over time roles take hold and become really difficult to break away from. Whereas in the early days we all swapped our instruments around and sang when we felt like it, by our third album I was the singer and guitarist, D was the bass player and Paul was the drummer. We also fell into personality traps. I was the stressed-out, wisecracking one. D was the organized, serious one. Paul was the calm, ingeniously creative one. These identities started to chafe. We fought constantly. And things were complicated by other problems in our lives. We had proper relationships, but none of us had proper jobs. It was starting to worry us. We argued our way through the production of our third and final album.

We stayed friends. We got through it. We called the record *Let's Work It Out*. When you start a band you're basically hooking your hopes and aspirations to other people. This is a lovely thing when you're in your rootless and directionless twenties. I got to spend ten years making things with people I loved. And when I listen to the music we made now – all three albums of it – it feels like it was someone else. It's not me. It's the product of a hive mind I can no longer tap into.

The NPB came to an end in 2004, but it really ended in 2010, when Paul died. The three of us had started playing music together again. Paul had just completed an album of his own. My last conversation with him was about music. Two days later, at seven in the morning, my phone rang. It was D telling me that Paul was dead. There was something wrong with his heart. That's a bigger tragedy than can be contained in a story about a minor Dublin indie band. That's a bigger story than I can tell, to be honest with you.

Upstairs in my attic I have hundreds of cassette tapes. On those tapes are interviews and eight-track recordings and rough mixes and proposed track listings for albums. On many of them, between the guitar hum and snare hits there are snippets of forgotten conversations, laughter, arguments, non-sequiturs and the beginnings of crazy schemes. I started playing them recently. More than our albums, listening to those tapes is like listening to being twenty-five, to being in a band. After a while I had to stop. It was three young men talking about music in the 1990s. Their conversations were bigger than I could handle. Their dreams were bigger than I could handle. I'm a different person now. I'm not in a band. I don't know if I'll listen to them again.

Brain Fever

(A catalogue of mental-health difficulties)

Loneliness

When I was a child we moved away from our home in Cork to live on an army base, where my father worked as a commando and I did not fit in.

I tried to impress people. I wandered around the streets in an archaic army helmet, weighed down with military water bottles and canvas bags, hoping someone would ask me about them. It didn't occur to me that, on an army base, no one would be impressed by army gear.

For a while I played with younger children and was pleased to feel suddenly good at sport until some bigger boys mocked me for rugby-tackling a four-year-old neighbour. They laughed. I slapped one of them. They punched me in the head. Some time later I walked into a swarm of bees to impress them. It impressed no one.

I was befriended at one point by two other boys, but it turned out they had really befriended my yellow Lego castle, which they regularly called around to play with.

'Those boys are using you,' said my mother, who is no fool, so one day I told her to tell them that I wasn't in.

'Can we still come in and play with his yellow Lego castle?' they said.

She said 'No,' but I could tell she was nearly swayed by their chutzpah. They were more charismatic than me.

Something had to be done. I sent a letter anonymously to the older boy, challenging him to meet me at a hollow in the Curragh Plains, to which I planned to turn up in disguise. 'My name doesn't matter!' I would say from a height in a deep superhero voice, wearing my dad's paramilitary balaclava and overcoat, which would make me look taller and wider than I was. 'The important thing is that you have to be nice to Patrick from now on.' Dramatic pause. 'Or I'll get you.'

Only after sneaking up and sticking my invitation through the letterbox of the boy's house did I realize that his family was away on holiday. Then I forgot about our secret assignation until one day, a few weeks later, I found the neighbourhood kids sitting around discussing it. Not knowing that it came from me, they were hypothesizing about which local girl it was from. They had read it as a sort of love letter. I suppose it was.

I gained some status eventually. I became fourth-toughest boy in fifth class at the local National School by allowing myself to be repeatedly punched in the face by John Leahy (second toughest) until, frustrated by the fact he couldn't make me cry, he burst into tears himself. This feat, admired by many, saw Dodo Kilkenny (first toughest) promote me to fourth toughest at the expense of Conor Adams. Dodo's word was law and I was secretly pleased to have ascended the ranks without having to hit anyone myself. Hitting people hurt my fists.

I realized at this point that my best option for fitting in was to be a bit kooky, a bit odd, to be the sort of person who doesn't give a hoot about being punched in the face. My favourite television programme was *The A-Team*. I liked 'Howling Mad' Murdock, the pilot with PTSD whom the others repeatedly sprang from a mental-health institution in order to save a village from loggers or bandits or predatory capitalism. And so for a while a mentally ill TV character became a role model for me.

Bereavement

When I was twenty-one my schoolfriend Barry died from an infection of the brain. It was a fluke event. Intrepid bacteria permeated a tiny undiscovered skull fracture and ultimately stopped his funny mind and warm heart. I'd been to visit him in the hospital the day before he died, only to find him hooked up to machines and his family gathered about him. They left me alone with him for a moment, but I didn't know what to say. I said nothing and regretted it instantly. His sister rang me on our house phone the next day to tell me that he was dead.

I didn't feel sad – that came later. I felt an absence of feeling, and that scared me terribly. After the phone call, I wandered out of our housing estate down the main road that ran from Newbridge to the Curragh Camp, over a rusting gate into the scraggly fields beyond our house. There was an old tree there that the local kids called the Talking Tree after an incident in which a teenager hid in its branches and scared a younger simpleton by intoning, 'I am the Talking Tree!' The child became hysterical and rumour spread about the tree's powers and its new name. So we climbed that tree all the time. There was a method to it. You had to find certain hand-holds and knots and branches and hoist and haul your way up. I can't describe it properly now, but if you resurrected that tree – because that tree is also dead now – I could do it with muscle memory.

It was a windy, grey day in 1996. The branches shook as I ascended and near the top I clung on to the trunk and looked across the field. And I stayed there for a while thinking about Barry and I was suddenly terrified of falling. I could fall and die. At twenty-one I realized you could die in a stupid, meaningless way. This knowledge was absolutely useless to me the next time I lost someone that I loved.

Hypochondria

Recently I found a note in an old pocket. 'Numb feeling on left side of head. Burning itchy patch on scalp. Red sore eyes. Sharp pain under right arm. Pins and needles in feet. Occasional stomach upset. Bad dreams. Floaters on my vision (I can't quite see them). Red rash on chest. Erratic heartbeat.'

It was a note to take to my doctor. I have many such notes hidden away in faded charity-shop jackets. By my late twenties my neurosis and grief had blossomed into full-blown hypochondria and my middle-aged doctor began greeting me like an old friend or, probably more accurately, a silent business partner who was helping put his children through college.

There was never anything wrong with me and I spent hundreds each month on doctors and scans and tests that always turned out to be negative. I never had a drug habit or a flashy lifestyle. For a while I spent my meagre earnings on medical tests instead.

And then I got broadband, which taught me new facts about life. Did you know that every feeling you have in your body is also potentially a symptom of terminal cancer? It took me several years to realize the futility of my cyber-chondria. Then in my thirties I was pleased/appalled to discover that there were several serious hereditary diseases running in my family.

So fuck you, I was dying all along. (I'm joking. I'll probably be fine.)

Fear of God

For a couple of years in my late teens I would go with Barry's lovely family to a summertime retreat for Charismatic Catholics in the Burren. Charismatic Catholicism was for Catholics who really wanted to be evangelical Protestants. They weren't in it for the judgement or the conformity or the sense of inherited propriety, or to meet Deirdre from down the road or to get the paper afterwards, or any of the other reasons Irish Catholics typically flaunt the faith. They were in it for the rush of God's grace as it coursed through their veins. They were in it for the regular fix of divinity dispensed, like medicine, via the Eucharist. They wanted a personal relationship with Jesus, but also incense and transubstantiation and all the other good stuff that comes with the universal Church.

I was, by then, a greasy-haired indie kid in a parka, and despite my wavering faith I enjoyed the painful barefoot walk up a stony road to the sparse wooden church where a gentle priest would talk with a breaking voice about the passion of Christ. He told us to contemplate the beautiful brutalized body of Christ on the cross, and I did. 'He's so human,' he said, with tears in his eyes.

People would have strange turns and speak in tongues occasionally, but this was seen as a bit attention-seeking, a bit low-rent, by the regulars. Most of the congregation just basked in God's undeniable love for them. I did so myself. I have felt God's love, which is a strange thing to remember now.

In the evenings we teenagers sat around tents in the sand dunes, eating toasted egg sandwiches and playing guitars while trying to get off with one another. Barry and I harmonized on badly remembered Violent Femmes songs about teenage lust and one night, after kissing a pair of deeply religious Cavan girls, we walked amid squalls of rain on the rocky, sea-battered coast watching the sun come up. Barry was the first person I saw the sun rise with. I think of us there often, the two of us at the edge of the world with the rain on our faces.

On the last night I spent in Clare, Barry's sister and I drank a bottle of whiskey together, after which she hid me from the adults in her tent and held my hair as I vomited up the last of my religion on the sand. 'You're hilarious,' she said, which I took as a compliment.

A few years later, a few years after Barry had died, his brother invited me to go to a prayer meeting in a red-brick Georgian townhouse on Bachelors Walk. A woman would be speaking. A healer. A mystic. And, because I was twenty-four and didn't have anything better to do, I went along.

I sat in the back of the room. Barry's brother, a serene skateboarder who would later join a religious order, sat beside me with his eyes shut and his palms open and facing upwards. Others did likewise, though some joined their hands. I was wary and didn't shut my eyes. The mystic was middle-aged with short grey hair, a pink knitted jumper and guarded grey eyes. Amid group recitation of prayer – that comforting, hurried blur of doctrine – she would walk among the twenty or so people present and, occasionally, stop short and whisper something into someone's ear. The person would then express great joy or would begin to cry softly. One woman gasped and brought her hand to her mouth before doing both.

The message was clear. This woman knew things. She knew things that she couldn't possibly know about these people she had never met. She caught my eye and I became very frightened that she would stop and say something to me, something terrible and huge that would make me re-evaluate my atheistic worldview or my place in the universe, or a secret of Fatima or the true and terrifying nature of the cherubim.

And then I became convinced she would tell me something even worse, something unknowable and unprovable that would niggle at me for ever – like the time and place of my death or that I had a secret brother or sister. That smiling woman in her bright pink jumper made me feel scared.

And so I got up and, without saying anything to Barry's brother, I left. If God existed, I didn't want to know. I didn't miss the terror of God until years later, when my mother was diagnosed with cancer and I faced, again, the terror of nothing.

OCD

Once, long ago, I became obsessed with the idea I might kill a loved one for no reason. My girlfriend. My mother. My sister. My brother. One of my friends. I lay in bed awake at night imagining doing something I didn't want to do. I couldn't stop thinking about it – about the act, the aftermath, the consequences, my grief.

I couldn't socialize and I couldn't relax. The manner in which I feared killing them was cartoonish and born of watching too many action movies: I would simply reach over for no reason when they were sleeping/driving/sitting beside me in a car or a café or a kitchen and I would snap their neck with my bare hands. The mode of death was very specific. It was the worst thing I could imagine happening.

I went to a psychologist. He asked me why I worried about killing my girlfriend, mother, brother, sister and friends but didn't worry about killing my father. I explained that my father was a former army ranger and that he'd be able to neutralize me before I got anywhere near enough to snap his neck with my bare hands. The psychologist told me that I wasn't Jean-Claude Van Damme and couldn't just snap someone's neck with my bare hands. I was a bit hurt by this. He also pointed out that I clearly didn't really have any desire to kill the people I loved but just had a compulsive fear that I would. That made me feel better.

Then he started talking about once testifying on behalf of a man who'd killed his spouse because she had 'nagged' him so much. He said it to console me, but it actually made me feel worse, because a) it made it feel possible that I still might kill someone after all and b) I didn't want to get off prison for institutionally misogynistic reasons.

One way or another, I eventually stopped fearing that I might kill people I loved. Is it possible that I just got tired of it? That's what it felt like. It's actually quite difficult to remain intensely worried all the time. Years later I realized that what I was experiencing – unpleasant intrusive thoughts – were a symptom of obsessive compulsive disorder.

This made sense. As a self-important small child, I was obsessed with having my sleeve cuffs rolled up the exact same way on both arms and would have screaming tantrums if this wasn't the case.

The obsessive thoughts about murdering loved ones never recurred. Thank God. That was undoubtedly the worst time of my life.

Hypochondria II, some more context

My hypochondria, I had always told myself, had been triggered by Barry's death. I traced all my fears to a dawning sense of my own mortality, sitting alone in a tree, in a field, in County Kildare.

'That's not true,' said my friend Paul one day. 'In London you were convinced you were having a brain haemorrhage and wouldn't shut up about it.'

A year before Barry died, Paul recalled, Paul and I had been wandering the streets of London after returning from our squalid summer of service jobs and mild substance abuse in Germany. I got a blinding flash of pain in my right temple and behind my eye and, according to Paul's account, I spent a whole day 'moaning and wailing' and convinced I needed to go to hospital.

He did not make it sound like the intriguing behaviour of a troubled eccentric, more like the whingeing of an annoying toddler. Paul did not think I needed to go to hospital. At one point, he said, I put some massage oil on my forehead, poured it into my eye by mistake and started to cry.

That does sound like me.

So Barry's death did not trigger my hypochondria. Damn

it. Neat narratives are generally lies. I don't know where my hypochondria comes from.

I think I know when it ended, though this is also a bit neat. Paul did not suffer from hypochondria. By the time he died without warning at thirty-five, I'm not sure how much he'd thought about death. He told me years before that it never crossed his mind. He was a professional psychotherapist by then, having tested his skills over the years on his more neurotic friends. When he died, he was in the middle of counselling a nurse who had come for existential solace and got more than she bargained for. She performed CPR, but she couldn't revive him.

He was a kind of genius, Paul. If he were here, he would note that I was making his death, like Barry's, all about myself. I miss him.

Narcissism

It's an odd feeling when you realize your therapist doesn't like you. I spent the final month of a half-year's worth of weekly sessions with Janet (not her real name) trying to convince her that I was actually tormented and not just pretending to be.

'Those feelings are quite normal, really, given your workload,' she'd say.

'Oh, I dare say you'd feel a lot better after a night's sleep,' she'd say.

'Maybe you're just hungry? Have you eaten?' she'd ask.

Janet spent a lot of time trying to rationalize my feelings away, while I'd try to convince her that they were real. 'Is it not meant to be the other way around?' I'd think, but, because I'm a stickler for authority, I'd also think, 'Well, she's the therapist!'

I should have guessed the nature of our relationship early on. The slightly disappointed look on her face when she came out on a Tuesday evening and saw me in the waiting room. The way she once explained what would happen if we bumped into one another on the street: she would pretend not to know me.

I knew about this practice. It's common for counsellors to do this as a way of maintaining the confidentiality of the therapy room. But Janet went to very great pains to outline the various locations in which she might pretend not to recognize me – in the street, in the supermarket, out at the theatre, while I was performing CPR on her after plucking her from the sea (I made up the last one). Even at the time I felt that she was taking a bit too much pleasure in this. She seemed to be more worried about her boundaries than about mine.

The point of therapy, I'd always thought, was it was the place where you could voice the shameful buried feelings you had about your loved ones without being judged. With Janet I'd begin outlining my dark secrets and when I looked up at her I'd see her looking slightly bored.

I have heard decent critiques of psychotherapy, about how counsellors can often reinforce someone's self-identified victimhood when they don't really have access to the full picture. Counsellors are too willing to take their client's side. Not Janet. Sometimes I wondered if she was a therapist at all. Perhaps I had simply wandered into the wrong room one day and begun unburdening myself to a podiatrist. If so, she had decided to roll with it and take her seventy quid a session.

The anxiety attacks and bouts of deadening depression that had initially led me to enter therapy were, at the time, getting worse. She had a simple solution to this: she told me they were getting better.

I guess I should have stopped going to see her. Instead I entered into a self-destructive battle of wills. For about a month before we finally stopped, each session would start with her explaining how I had made a lot of progress. I would then spend the duration of the session explaining to her how I was actually feeling worse than ever.

In retrospect, it seems clear that Janet thought I was a self-pitying dick and was trying to end the therapy. I think I sensed this even at the time, but one of my fatal flaws is that I always want to be liked.

For example, I remember an art class in secondary school during which a friend and I stapled the sides of our jumpers together in order to pretend to be conjoined twins. We were kicked out of class. The next day I went out of my way to try to make the art teacher like me again by being particularly interested in the Renaissance. He saw exactly what I was doing. 'You are such an asshole,' he hissed, which was the first time I ever heard a teacher swear.

When I was even younger I was sent off to the Gaeltacht,

where I thought the best route to popularity was to become a lickspittle for the older, cooler, Dublin boys. I would do errands for them and laugh at their jokes. I recall with burning shame the day one of those boys sent me to fetch his guitar in front of some pretty girls, just to show them that he could order me about. I got the guitar. What else was I going to do?

I want to be liked. There's a talented young writer out there who once wrote something disparaging about my writing style on an internet forum, and subsequently every time I meet him at events I bend over backwards to impress on him how well read, countercultural and generally clued in I am.

It's pathetic, really. Janet's apparent dislike triggered something in me and, despite knowing that the sessions were doing nothing for me, I kept going in order to change her mind. It's no wonder she didn't like me. Reading this, I don't like me.

Sometimes, looking back, I think that Janet's approach to therapy – suggesting to people that they are not mentally ill but just a bit rubbish – may actually be a good one. Maybe this is the deep realization dawning at the edge of most mental crises; maybe we should just go with it . . . 'Ah, I see now. I'm kind of crap.' Maybe that's what they call a 'breakthrough'.

I asked a therapist friend of mine what therapists do when faced with a client they simply don't like. 'Oh, we try and hide it,' he said. 'I'm not sure we always succeed.'

Depression

You know how on airplanes babies cry because of the air pressure and someone says, 'It's worse for babies because they don't know what's going on'?

Well, when they say that I always think, 'But that's how I feel all the time. I want to burst into tears because I also don't have a clue what's going on. Does everyone else know what's going on? Is that what's wrong with me? Does everyone else know what's going on?'

And when I see a child having a full-on tantrum in a supermarket I also think, 'Yes! That's what I want to do! I want to do that. I want to lie down there on the ground and kick and scream and thrash.' I look at the exasperated parents of the child and think, 'Why are they being so judgemental? Don't they want to lie down there on the ground and kick and scream and thrash too? Don't we all want to do that? Isn't that the dream?'

Because every few days the world is out of alignment – its sleeves don't match up and its seams aren't straight and the lights are too bright and the tannoy is crackly and hurts my ears.

The world isn't black, which is a shame because I wanted to be a goth when I was younger; no, the world is colourful, but the colours of this world are stupid and badly matched and they make my ears ring and my throat gag. On those days, I don't see the point of anything.

On those days, I would like to buck my body and bend

my knees and erupt into a series of unchoreographed yells and jerks that finally end in a long shriek so inconsolable and irrational that passers-by think, 'Someone should really do something about that.'

In my imagining, the passers-by stare at my wife, or, if things have gone really badly, my mother, and think, 'Why don't you do something about him?', because it's obvious that I'm too far gone to do anything about myself. And then they bring their gaze back over to me, and by now I'll be literally gnawing the supermarket's floor in rage and sadness, and they shake their heads.

And then, before I know it, big arms will pick me up, God's arms maybe, or a paramedic's arms more probably, and they'll take me somewhere where I can rest.

That's a fantasy of mine when things are bad.

Things get bad frequently enough – usually when I take a break and I retreat into myself. Without the compulsive stress of work deadlines, I am overwhelmed by choices. I become an anxious wreck – a boiling stew of self-loathing, an endless series of fruitless, pointless options. I don't want to be alone. I don't want to be with others. I don't want to think of the future. I am mortified by the past. Everything is too loud. Everything is too bright. My head hurts. I am exhausted. I am hateful. And underneath this swirling mess of thoughts, when my mind is clear enough to perceive it, there's a numb and throbbing sadness.

Brain fever

I prefer older categorizations of mental frailty. I have read biographies about nineteenth-century polymaths who suffered from 'neurasthenia' and who regularly retired to bed with phantom illnesses and 'brain fevers' and 'nerve disorders', afflictions that were apparently consequential of their superior sensitivity and brilliance. 'Brain fever' always seems to more accurately describe how I feel when I'm depressed, I think, than any modern diagnosis.

I'd love to use such language with the HR department where I work whenever I feel the way I sporadically feel. It would be way cooler than saying 'I get panic attacks and would prefer to stay in bed' or 'I just feel really sad today' or 'Existence is hard.'

Mental-health issues are for everybody now. Our collective psychic pain has become almost boring, and our different diagnoses seem prosaic and clinical, and writing about them isn't taboo or exotic any more. I'm not complaining.

OK, I am complaining, because I want to be special, but I know that complaining makes no sense.

Still, sometimes I long to go backwards. I would love to be seen through privileged nineteenth-century eyes as an ethereal scholar in a top hat on some higher plane of intellectual exertion in dire need of an expensive rest cure, some shock therapy or a bit of laudanum.

There's a delusion that I'm told some people have: that they are the only sentient being in the universe and that everyone else is an automaton or a hologram, senselessly enacting some cosmic play. I know one of these people, as it turns out. My friend D, on an early date with his now wife, alarmed her by telling her that he did not believe she existed. His now wife, a sensible person, had never heard the like. 'Now,' he says, 'we just don't bring up the fact I don't believe she exists.' There's a lesson here about how to maintain a happy marriage.

Personally, I have no problem with the fact that D doesn't believe I exist, because a) he's very kind to the people he doesn't believe exist and b) I sort of agree with him. But I have a very different intuition about my own existence than D has about his. I have a recurring fear that I'm not as sentient as other people, that I can't experience reality as fully or completely as they can. That I'm not processing things correctly. That my reality has downloaded at a lower resolution. That I'm not all there.

The brilliant thing about this, as a sustainable fear that will ride with me to the grave, is that I can never know for sure. And neither can you. We can never know for sure.

Care

Once upon a time I was a carer.

It was at the height of the Celtic Tiger, a time when it was difficult to fill these positions. A relative of mine worked in an institution that looked after intellectually disabled adults, and that institution needed people to come and look after some of the very vulnerable people in their care. I was in college doing a postgraduate degree in music at the time, after spending most of my twenties trying to be a musician, and I was a bit lost and in need of money.

The campus was made up of one austere red-brick Victorian building and a number of more modern bungalows and buildings in which people lived and were cared for. The institution had historically looked after women only, but in more recent decades it had begun looking after men as well. Because there was a particularly acute shortage of male staff, I was put to work at first in the only bungalow inhabited entirely by young men.

The people we worked with were called 'clients'. Their disabilities were classified as 'mild', 'moderate', 'severe' and 'profound', and in this bungalow there were seven clients with very different combinations of intellectual and physical difficulties to contend with. Some used wheelchairs and were unable to walk. About half of them couldn't talk. One young man could say three things: 'Uh oh!', 'Hello' and 'Fuck off'. I later learned that knowing one swearword and few other words isn't that unusual for intellectually disabled people. Curses have power. I think if I was largely non-verbal, 'fuck' would be a word I'd gravitate towards. ('Hello' and 'uh oh' seem pretty useful too.)

Every morning, the routine was the same. Clients would be bathed or showered and given breakfast. It was physically demanding. Some people had to be lifted from beds to wheelchairs to shower chairs or baths or toilets. You had to be strong but gentle with a small young man who had scoliosis, and you had to be careful, too, of stronger young men who threw their arms out suddenly and without warning.

After the bath or shower, you helped to dress and change them. People who have never done care work before are obsessed with the notion of changing adult nappies. They assume that this is the most difficult thing about the job. On my first day a young man I was looking after had diarrhoea in the bath; after that, nappy changes were no problem. It's just poo.

Breakfasts were more difficult. Some of the clients could feed themselves. Others had to be fed. One young man could feed himself but needed to be monitored in case he took a Kit-Kat from the treat tin and hid it beneath his Weetabix and milk. I understood his urge to do this. He lived in an environment that was highly controlled and this was a bit of rebellion. Also, if you like Weetabix and you like Kit-Kats, who's to say they don't go well together?

Another young man had epilepsy and often had fits

during breakfast. He had to wear a helmet all the time in case he hit the ground hard. When he had these seizures, his cornflakes would fly across the room and he would quiver and shake. I would rush over to make sure he didn't bang his head. While it was happening, he would get an expression on his face that was beatific. It looked like he was having a religious experience. Afterwards he would be confused and fuzzy for the whole day and I'd wonder what he'd seen.

After breakfast the residents would all go out to day-care centres around the campus aimed at people with different levels of need. Sometimes I went to work in the day-care centre for more severely disabled people, some of whom were fully grown adults but with lives not much different from those of babies. They were fed and changed and read to and wheeled around. I sometimes brought my guitar to play music for them. I remember a young woman who would lean her head against the body of the guitar and put her hand to the wood, feeling the vibrations as I played.

Young men from backgrounds like mine are encouraged to be ambitious and clever and, maybe, in a slightly detached manner, to be kind. We're taught abstract notions like 'ethics'. But we're not conditioned to nurture or care. The most socially respectable approach to care for the middle classes is to earn enough money to pay other people to do it. So, with all that in mind, it's a beautiful thing when you realize that it's something you can do: to physically care for a stranger.

In the afternoon, everyone would return to the bungalows and we would find ways to pass the time. We went for drives to shopping centres and parks. We read aloud from books.

One young man liked to go for walks, but he also liked to bolt in the direction of traffic, and I got very used to people staring when I was trying to stop him from running across the road. I first realized that embarrassment was a useless emotion when I was working as a care worker. What strangers think of you is not useful information when you're trying to stop someone from being hit by a bus.

Another young man spent a lot of his time playing a Casio keyboard that was set up in his room. I had been studying atonal music, and a lot of his stuff was in the same ballpark. I preferred his take on it, to be honest. It had more heart. He had a loving family to whom he went home every weekend. The only problem was that he couldn't tell when it was the weekend and it was hard to explain this to him. Sometimes, in the middle of the week, he would lay out his best clothes on his bed and would stare out the window looking for his father's car. Eventually, he would put a Carpenters CD into his stereo and lie on the bed and cry very quietly to himself. He had realized it wasn't Friday or, and this broke my heart, he thought that they had abandoned him.

A third boy liked to get out of his wheelchair, drag himself across the floor and upend things. He was a gleeful lord of chaos. I once made the mistake of seating him in the car seat behind me, enabling him to yank my hair violently just as I was trying to negotiate a roundabout. He tended to erupt into joyously wheezing laughter whenever he successfully achieved something he had set out to do. That day

I thought that that laugh would be the last thing I ever heard. There are worse ways to go. He had an excellent sense of comic timing, that kid. Also, I had a perfectly grabbable ponytail, something no man should have, so I was definitely asking for it.

Some of the other clients would throw plastic crockery or slap you across the head when you weren't looking. In another life, some of them might well have been arms dealers or commodities traders. And in another life, some of them might have been nurses and care workers themselves. But it wasn't another life. It was *this* life. They were all vulnerable and they all did what they could while I fed, changed and entertained them. That was my job.

Some young men went home every weekend. Some had visits a few times a week. One hadn't had a family visit in a year. Many of their families had had to facilitate a lifetime of under-resourced care, and I couldn't honestly say what I'd do in those circumstances. There were many cases in which one parent had disappeared, never to be seen again, while the other devoted their life to making sure their child was OK. Caring is full on: you are constantly carrying and lifting and trying to understand and to be understood. I always had the option of leaving it all behind at the end of a working day, but people caring for a disabled family member at home did not.

I knew this, but it didn't stop me from occupying the moral high ground during political discussions with left-wing friends. 'As a care worker . . .' I would say, in the same way some people say, 'As a mother . . .' Friends said things like, 'You're so good,' and I said, 'Oh no, I'm not,' even though I secretly thought, 'I am good. I'm a saint.' And many of them said, 'I don't think I could do that,' and I thought, 'Yeah, you flake, you'd be totally unable to do this.'

I liked the job. It was gruelling and sometimes boring, but it was also straightforwardly, uncomplicatedly useful. If someone was in discomfort, you eased their discomfort. If someone was dirty, you cleaned them. If someone was bored, you entertained them. There was nothing abstract about it. If you did your job badly, people suffered. If you did your job well, someone might have a good day. For possibly the first time in my life I had no doubt in my mind that I was contributing to society. I slept better than I had in years, and better than I ever have since.

After a while, I was asked to work in the behavioural unit. The clients in this bungalow had thick files that outlined multiple diagnoses and had long lists of medication. They needed more one-on-one care and supervision. At the old unit, I was slapped or scratched or had my hair pulled from time to time, but I never saw anything I'd actually call 'violence'. In the behavioural unit there was violence.

Often before an incident you could feel a strange energy in the air. I've experienced it since as a journalist – talking to far-right activists or sad, unpredictable drug addicts – but I think working in the behavioural unit attuned me to it. When danger is imminent, I can feel my spine going cold and the hairs on my neck prickle with something like static electricity. When we feel that electricity, I believe on some level we're reading someone else's body language or their pulse rate or adrenalin levels. The perpetrator of future violence is trying to tell us what's about to occur. They're trying to tell us that they have as little control over the situation as we have. They're warning us.

The most dangerous client was Robert. When each of my nephews reached the age of six they reminded me of Robert. He was sweet and curious and funny, but every now and again something would shift for him and he would lash out violently, running at staff and hitting them with big arms and badly made fists. He didn't know how to make a fist. It wasn't his fault he was big.

He could do a lot of damage. The recommended tactic for dealing with violence in the unit was always de-escalation and containment. We were rightly forbidden from grabbing limbs or restraining people. It was their home, after all. We just worked there. But de-escalation is a very difficult thing to achieve. It's hard to speak soothing words to someone who is throwing punches at you while you are simultaneously trying to keep someone more vulnerable out of their path.

I didn't always react to this violence as I expected I would. I had spent my childhood imagining myself disarming terrorists and armed bank robbers with hitherto unsuspected bravery and skill. But when I saw Robert get a young nurse down on to the floor by the back of her neck, and then kneel on her back while pulling her arm backwards, I froze. I was trying to keep another client out of Robert's way. But the fact is, I just stood there, holding the client back as the nurse started to panic and cry.

Two other staff members rushed past me. If they hadn't been there, I've no idea what might have happened. After such outbreaks of violence, I usually felt an adrenalized sense of alert that took hours to subside. After that incident I also felt shame. I still feel a flush of shame when I think about it now.

The other residents were less dangerous, mainly because they weren't as big. They included Claudia, who was usually very calm but was often disturbed by the presence of new staff and would respond by stuffing all her clothes down the toilet then running at people, hitting out and throwing things.

Then there was Kate, who had a sense of humour and liked to do errands. She had a book with stars stuck to it to indicate her good behaviour. This was a good system. Who doesn't want to get gold stars in their book? I know many people who could do with a book like Kate's to keep them on the straight and narrow. For Kate, bad behaviour involved upending tables and punching people. She was related to a Dublin gangland figure. When at home, a colleague told me, she had a freedom she didn't have here, walking the streets on her own if she so chose.

'But is she safe on her own?' I asked once.

'Who'd touch her with that surname?' said my colleague.

Let's be clear, it was nice and calm there most of the time. It reminds me a bit of Charlie Watts's quip about how being the drummer in the Rolling Stones had involved about a year of drumming and twenty years of waiting around. Most days in the behavioural unit were a picture of genteel domesticity. We mopped floors, made beds, prepared meals, coloured in colouring books, went for walks and watched the same Michael Jackson, Abba and Daniel O'Donnell DVDs over and over again.

I made Robert and Kate laugh and they made me laugh. And the other staff made me laugh too. They had a sort of warm gallows humour that, if you were to put examples in an essay, could get the best and most loving ones fired.

Those best and most loving ones were almost always working-class women from Dublin or Lagos or Manila for whom 'care' was a core value, not just a job. These are the people who say, 'Are you OK, love?' to the stranger who is crying on the bus. They care before they can stop themselves. I try to be like these people, but it's not easy. They're not well paid for this approach to life. They're basically punished for it. In contrast, I know someone whose job at a multinational is to make employees feel so uncomfortable that they leave. That man will be rich enough to retire when he's fifty.

At some point my manager decided to put me in a unit that housed just one woman named Julie. A lot of the staff didn't particularly like working with Julie because Julie didn't like working with most of the staff. Julie was a small thirty-something with Down's syndrome. She couldn't share a unit with anyone else because, when she did so, she would sneak out of her bedroom at night and crawl along the corridor to other people's rooms, where she would then scratch their faces as they slept.

She didn't like people. The first thing Julie did when

someone new came in the door of her apartment was to throw a shoe at their forehead. She was really good at this. She was so good I sometimes had to restrain myself from giving her a round of applause when she brained someone. I also got really good at ducking.

Julie's living room featured nothing that could be picked up and thrown. There was a stereo, but it was in a high cupboard that Julie could not reach.

When I first arrived she was regularly cared for by agency staff, the people who are called in when the high rates of sick leave necessitated it. There's a high rate of sick leave in jobs like this.

Agency staff were a problem. Often they were there for just one day and didn't know the clients they worked with. They'd usually never met anyone like Julie before. They would hear fearful tales and would then sit on the other side of the room while Julie glowered at them from a beanbag. Forgetting, for a moment, that that's an unkind way to deal with a vulnerable woman, it's also a very boring way to spend a twelve-hour shift.

In contrast, if Julie got used to you and you did the things that interested her, you could have a pretty pleasant day. Here's one of the things Julie liked to do: she liked to make her own breakfast. Agency staff worried that she would throw the breakfast things, so they didn't let her do this. I let her make breakfast and she rarely threw things. Instead she put ridiculous combinations of marmalade and cheese on brown bread and then put the bread on pink plastic plates and ate it all, looking thrilled with herself.

'I have to say, Julie, that wouldn't be my preferred breakfast,' I'd say.

'Nice breakfast,' she'd say, swallowing it with pride.

She liked to play cards. By this I mean that she had a deck of cards and she would solemnly hand them to me one by one. When I had them all in my hands, I would then solemnly start handing them back to her. To be honest with you, this wasn't that much more tedious than any of the 'poker nights' I've had with friends.

She liked to be talked to. So I would tell her about my plans for the evening and I might narrate whatever she was doing or whatever I was doing. Sometimes I would tell her what I knew about the recording of my favourite albums: 'So when Steve Albini was first introduced to the music of The Pixies . . .' Sometimes I would tell her plots of films I had seen: 'So Frodo and Sam were on their way to Mordor.' All that mattered to Julie was that I was focusing my words on her. I often went home hoarse.

She loved to go on the trampoline in the garden. The only problem was she would insist I go on it too. I was very, very unfit at the time because I hadn't yet realized that 'exercise' wasn't just a scam perpetuated by jocks and squares on the rest of us.

'Jump,' she would say, as I lay wheezing on the grass.

'Give me a minute,' I'd wheeze.

'Patrick, jump.'

She was very fit. She was such a good gymnast that when she was younger she'd been considered a serious Special Olympics contender. This was probably why she was so good at kicking and throwing things. And then, the kicking and the throwing were the reasons she had to stop going to gymnastics, which made her sad and more likely to kick and throw things.

She liked to go out on a large adult-sized tricycle that someone had donated to the centre. She would cycle around the sports field with me walking alongside her. Whenever someone passed, I would stand between her and them, while she muttered darkly to herself from the bike. 'Scratch her face,' she would say, and it was not just an empty threat.

'Better hurry on, I'm not sure I can stop her,' I'd say, if it was a staff member I didn't like.

Julie hated most people, but she was capable of loving one person at a time: that's how a colleague put it. I became that one person, and so Julie needed me to focus on her completely. If my attention wandered even slightly, she'd be upset. She would throw a cup or she would deliberately wet herself. Sometimes she would go for my face with her nails. I tried to keep her nails short, and when she was out and about I made sure she wore mittens, but I often went home with bright red scratches on my face. Once when we were out walking, she lay on the tarmacadam in a car park and refused to get up for over two hours. I had no phone. I had to just sit beside her, directing the occasional car around her, while she lay on her back singing gently to herself. Eventually, she got up, for no apparent reason, and started walking home.

'Home now,' she said impatiently, as I, stiff from sitting on the tarmacadam, tried to keep up with her.

Her acts of aggression were usually opportunistic. I once bent down to pick up some cards from the floor and she kicked me so hard in the throat that I blacked out for a moment. She hadn't even been angry with me. I had just been within kicking reach of her leg and she had been unable to resist. She burst into tears as soon as I fell. She often seemed instantly appalled by her own behaviour. She'd say, 'Julie very bold,' in her gravelly voice, and I would tell her that she wasn't bold, that she'd just done a bold thing. That was different, I said.

If she was feeling very melancholy she would lie back on her bean bag and ask for her *Best of Mary Black* CD to be put on the stereo. She would lie there, quietly listening and quietly crying. And then at the tenth song, 'A Song for Ireland', she would sing along, her voice breaking with emotion. She had a lot of emotion to get out and she used Mary Black to access it. A spell with Julie would teach a lot of music snobs what it means to really love art.

Julie had a history of abandonment. She'd been in a series of foster-care placements that had broken down. One had ended when the foster mother had had a baby of her own, and Julie simply couldn't cope with her divided attention. The last of her homes was with a wonderful woman who still visited her every week and took her out on drives. Julie *wanted* someone to be only for her.

What Julie *needed*, I think, was a consistent team of staff members who could help her get over this want. In a place based on shift work with a high turnover of staff and high demands elsewhere, that wasn't always possible. So when I was on shift, it was easier to put me with Julie than risk agency staff or someone that she wasn't accustomed to. This meant that when I wasn't on, Julie was more uncooperative than ever. On the mornings after I'd been away for a few days, I'd see actual joy on her face when I walked in the door. 'Patrick's here!' she'd say.

'God, can you feel that love?' a colleague once said. And I could. It was like sunlight.

When I left, there was no debriefing process. I wasn't full-time staff. I just started taking fewer shifts. I went from working four days a week to working two days a week to working none. I explained to Julie that I wouldn't be there for much longer, but I think that all she really understood was that one moment I was there and the next I was gone.

Over the years I've met a lot of people in caring professions, and here's something you can take for granted: they aren't paid enough. It is highly skilled work, but it isn't recognized as highly skilled by the type of people who determine how much people get paid. The best care workers have an ability to care for strangers that is positively virtuosic. But to acknowledge that would be to change how we organize the world. To give people who care for a living top status and top salaries would be a revolution.

Caring for a living can also be confusing. There's always going to be something troubling about a scenario in which someone's sense of security and affection comes from people who are paid to be there. For every day that I drove home from work with scratches and bruises, feeling like I'd earned my wages, there'd be another when I had experienced the simple force of someone else's love and it felt like I had stolen something.

I left and didn't come back, not for any philosophical or moral reason. I left simply because after a year or so working there I had started getting regular journalistic commissions. That's what, after a detour studying music, I had decided I wanted to do. In journalism, when you care, you care from a distance.

When I was a care worker, I did my best, I didn't do enough; I'm being hard on myself, I'm letting myself off lightly. All of these things feel true to me. For Julie, I became one more in a line of people who had abandoned her. And that's true too.

Workplace Culture in the Early Nineties

(A series of case studies for a future MBA)

My first experience of workplace culture was at the petrol station where my friend Corncrake worked when we were in our late teens. This was when you could just go and hang around with your friend when he was at work.

The owner of this particular petrol station was never there. He was an absentee owner, a non-interventionist deity whose creation ticked on without him. There was no manager, and the employees were all teenagers. Apart from Corncrake, there were two young stoners who I have decided to call, because they could well be barristers now, Calum and Clarence. Corncrake, Calum and Clarence dressed in grey overalls, much like the ones worn by Billy Joel and his dancing chums in the video for 'Uptown Girl'. However, this petrol station did not have a cameo appearance by Christie Brinkley. It had, instead, cameo appearances from me, a teenager so bored he would go and sit with his friend in a tiny booth while he worked on a Sunday.

The petrol was downwind of a shopping centre and across the green from a small, respectable-looking housing estate. Every Sunday, Corncrake would go down there, open up the garage, move some bales of briquettes around the place and then sit in the little cabin by the petrol pumps listening to the Pixies and waiting for people who needed petrol. By this time, humanity had figured out that people were capable of pumping their own petrol into their own cars. But the memo had apparently not reached this particular filling station, and so there was still a job for a sullen teenager in overalls.

The petrol station had a car-repair garage which usually wasn't operating when Corncrake was working there, but it doubled as a store for the peat briquettes that people often bought with their petrol. In the garage there was a little van thing (I remember it as being an electric van, but it probably wasn't an electric van because that sounds anachronistic), which was used to move briquettes around the place. Calum or Clarence, when they were there, enjoyed zipping around the petrol station on this little van, stoned off their gourds.

Occasionally, they would careen into the cabin in which Corncrake and I sat. Once, Corncrake told me, they had driven the little van into one of the petrol pumps. Another time, a car drove off, pulling a chunk of the petrol pump with it. Corncrake had fallen to his knees and thrown his hands over his head in anticipation of the ball of flame he felt sure was coming to claim him. A ball of flame did not claim him. Consequently, Corncrake felt immortal, and said it was OK for me to smoke in the booth.

Very few people came to the petrol station on a Sunday. Corncrake's main job, as it turned out, was to be on the lookout for his nemesis – a little blond-haired eight-year-old with milk-bottle-thick glasses who lived across the green. The blond-haired eight-year-old with milk-bottle glasses was obsessed with the pneumatic lift in the garage that was used to elevate the cars for repair purposes. The pneumatic lift was operated by some pretty self-explanatory big red buttons, and if I were an eight-year-old child I think I would have been pretty eager to press them myself.

Corncrake and I would be sitting in the booth contemplating existence and/or talking about girls when we'd hear a roaring engine sound.

'That little brat!' Corncrake would yell, and he'd be up and running for the garage, where the blond-haired eight-year-old with milk-bottle glasses would be looking up in awe as the elevator descended steadily down towards his soft, crushable head.

Then Corncrake would chase the eight-year-old child across the green shouting angrily, while the child laughed his head off. I'd wander back to the booth and wait.

'I hate that little fecker,' Corncrake would say again as he walked back towards the booth. We don't get to choose our enemies, and Corncrake's enemy happened to be the eight-year-old child from across the street.

'Why don't you just keep the garage door shut?' I'd say.

Corncrake would look at me like I was mad. 'Because we need to access the briquettes,' he'd say.

'Why don't you take a pile of briquettes out and put them in here in the booth and just open the garage as you need them?'

This question pained him. He just shook his head. I've learned since then that it's better to just listen to your loved ones' woes and not to be constantly trying to 'fix' them.

Unspoken between us was the understanding that chasing that eight-year-old child with milk-bottle glasses was Corncrake's real purpose here. This was his real job, just as it was Wile E. Coyote's real job to chase the Road Runner. It was an activity from which he garnered meaning. Who am I to hinder man's search for meaning?

Interestingly, there's been an equivalent of Corncrake chasing an eight-year-old across the green in every organization I've ever worked for, and there's also been the equivalent of someone who says, 'Why don't you just keep the door shut?' This is usually a know-nothing consultant who just doesn't get the institutional culture.

While Corncrake was working in the petrol station, I was working in a takeaway with a long kebab-related pun in the title. It was almost a decade after I left my post before I realized this name was actually a pun. When I worked there, I thought that it was an Arabic word meaning 'delicious food' or, because it was a small town in Ireland in the nineties, 'fight place' or, possibly, 'So this is it, then? The summit of my dreams.'

I was hired by a tired-looking Pakistani man named Ahmed who managed the franchise but was rarely there. I met him just twice. The first time I met him was on my first day when he explained at length how the cost of my uniform would be deducted from my salary packets and made me promise to stay for a long time because he kept losing workers. I lied and promised I would.

I was working alongside Cliff, a skinny bespectacled

thirty-something who took the job very, very seriously, and Michelle, who was the most sexually attractive racist I have ever met.

She had huge brown racist eyes and full red racist lips that were slightly upturned into a racist smile. She had a shaved racist head but she totally had the racist bone structure to carry it off.

I didn't know she was a racist then, so my first few weeks of work there were not remotely marred by such things. As far as I was concerned, Michelle was just another indie kid. Shaved heads were kind of cool at the time and she seemed to know some of the punk bands that my much hipper friend D had mentioned to me ('Oh yeah,' said D, when I later mentioned this to him. 'Some of those bands later became quite popular with racists.'). She also claimed to really like Bob Marley, which is still confusing to me.

This was an era in which teenage boys were born romantics. It was a time when I could transform any pretty face into a paragon of virtue and kindness. On Sunday I would go down to the petrol station where Corncrake worked and I would riff poetically about how funny and cool Michelle was and how nice her smile was while Calum drove the van around the forecourt in a fog of dope smoke and Corncrake sporadically chased an eight-year-old child across the green while screaming.

'What sort of things does she like?' Corncrake would ask.

'Music and World War II history,' I would say.

'She sounds nice,' Corncrake would say, wheezing in his oversized overalls.

She was nice. Very nice. I was certain of it.

Let me give you a quick account of a working night in a takeaway in a regional town in Ireland in the summer of 1994. My employers were purveyors of kebabs, a foodstuff that, as far as I know, has never turned up in an F. Scott Fitzgerald story or in the hand of James Bond. Nobody has ever said, 'Darling, the way you're shovelling that kebab into your vacant face in the neon light, it's quite enchanting. You're like a young Audrey Hepburn.'

Kebabs in Ireland consist of wet meat and veg crammed into a sort of soggy bread bag. Kebabs are the perfect drunken food, possibly because even when you eat them sober you start to feel like you're drunk. Your hand–eye coordination feels off. You get sauce on your cuffs. You find yourself picking bits of onion and pepper out of your hair. You can see, if you spend a bit of time watching people eating kebabs, that they are slipping into a sort of altered state.

In the early part of the evening we had regulars. There were two local 'characters', which is slightly too many for a small town. There was Chelsea, who wore a Chelsea football jersey and always wanted to talk about Chelsea FC, and then there was Michael Jackson, who dressed like Michael Jackson. He had a black hat, curly black hair, a white jacket, black slacks and black-and-white shoes. If you looked closely at the shoes, you could see that the white bits were done in Tipp-ex. He also had a microphone made out of cardboard, because he mimed to Michael Jackson songs on the street.

These men would sometimes purchase kebabs. If they were both there at the same time, they would sit on opposite ends of the counter because this town wasn't big enough for the both of them.

Then there was the terrifying couple who liked to start fights. Apparently, every small town has a couple like this. They'd seem completely placid and friendly until one of them would launch themselves at an unsuspecting kebab enthusiast and start slapping him or her across the head while the other shouted encouragement. 'That's what you get!' and 'Ha! Who's laughing now?', etc. Incidentally, the phrase 'Who's laughing now?' has never been said by anyone who is completely sane. Try saying it without an edge of hysteria in your voice. See? It's impossible.

When this terrifying couple were acting up, Cliff would sneak up the road to the police station to grab a guard, but the couple were wise to this. It was like a sixth sense. They'd suddenly stop tormenting whoever they were tormenting and stick their noses up in the air as though they'd felt a disturbance in the force. They'd always be gone by the time Cliff got back.

Once people had snaffled up their suppers there was usually a bit of a lull. If Cliff was on, this meant we'd have to do some stocktaking because Cliff, though not a racist, was a complete pain in the arse. Then Michelle and I would go out and smoke a cigarette and I would admire how she looked in the streetlights while she talked about Celtic heritage.

'How cultured she is!' I thought.

After this there would be a post-pub rush, at which point we were run off our feet. It was usually during the post-pub rush that Michelle's friends dropped in. They would be wearing knee-high Doc Martens and long military over-coats. Most of them had shaved heads. If Cliff wasn't there, Michelle gave them free food. 'They seem nice,' I thought.

Then there was another lull. If Cliff was there, he would do an extra-special counter wash and I would go back out-side to admire how Michelle held a cigarette as she discussed how she had, of late, become obsessed with the decadence of Weimar Germany.

'I like a girl who takes an interest in the world,' I thought.

Then the buses started to return. Here's a thing about my town in the early nineties. There was one nightclub in the town, but nobody seemed to go there, for reasons that largely amounted to 'a guy my brother knows was stabbed there last year'. This excuse rolled from year to year, so either the stabbing was an annual Wicker Man-style event (a possibility) or it was simply a small-town legend.

One way or another, from around ten every weekend evening fleets of minibuses took hordes of young people to nightclubs in nearby towns; and the same buses brought the young people back at around two in the morning, drunker and with a lot of energy to expend.

Tradition insists that violence in small towns needs an audience. Therefore, when the hordes descended for kebabs, the fights were typically kept to the street outside the shop to ensure that everyone could get a good look. There are two types of people in the world, and from behind a kebab-shop counter you can see both of them: there are those who run away from a fight and those who run towards it. If you are reading this, you're probably the first kind of person (but if you're the second, I've got something special planned for this book's launch party).

Around this point in the evening, drowning in pitta bread and garlic sauce and special meat, I had a tendency to burn myself quite badly. I remember one night picking up a metal device that was used to compress burgers but that had been accidentally left on the grill. It was red hot and stuck to my hand before dropping to the grill with a bit of my skin stuck to it. My hand was left with a red-and-white burn complete with welts.

'I think I need to go home,' I said, feeling woozy and feverish.

'No. Savlon will solve that,' said Cliff, and he went to get the Savlon.

'Don't listen to him,' said Michelle. She spat on my blisters. 'Saliva is good for wounds.'

'I'll never wash this hand,' I thought, but then I worried about getting an infection so I went and washed my hand.

After the nightclubs closed and the hordes had left or been dispersed, things went one of two ways. If Cliff wasn't working, we sprayed cleaning fluid on top of the mess (this is how I clean to this day) and went home. If Cliff was on, we stayed for an extra hour cleaning every surface before, if he was feeling really uptight, we did a complete stocktake of everything in the shop.

I don't *think* I'm a killer, but early one morning as the sun rose, standing alone outside a large freezer as Cliff shouted out numbers for me to write in a notebook, I found myself seriously contemplating locking him into the freezer and going home. If I had done such a thing, my life would probably be quite different now (possibly even better, who knows?).

It was a few weeks in, on a night much like the one described, that Michelle and I were sitting outside on the kerb smoking when Michelle turned to me and said, 'It's not a bad job, I just wish I wasn't working for *one of them*.'

My stomach flipped a bit at this point. Of course, I shouldn't have been so surprised. Not many teenage girls I knew had factoids about the Russian front or were so confident that they were a 'true Celt'. But I was naïve and in a kind of self-inflicted denial.

'Um, one of who?' I said.

She said some words I don't even like to type and there was no going back. It turned out that she listened to a lot of racist skinhead bands and believed in the sort of anti-Semitic conspiracy theories that were niche then but have been making a comeback recently.

I became angry. I told her that racism was stupid, which it is, but I'm not sure my argument was much more sophisticated than that at the time. I do remember saying: 'But you like Bob Marley?!' To which she said, inaccurately and confusingly, 'But Bob Marley knows his place.'

Yeah, she wasn't even a particularly well-informed racist. She also thought the Nazis had won the Battle of Stalingrad and that the Celts worshipped Thor. I had been willing to ignore these knowledge lapses before I knew she was a racist. Now, frankly, it was clear they were part of a bigger problem.

Over at the petrol station the next day, as Corncrake

scanned the horizon for his nemesis, I wondered aloud if I could patiently teach Michelle how to be not racist. 'I don't think you can,' said Corncrake gently, and he reminded me of how much these people would hurt anyone we knew who was different. Corncrake could often be quite wise. Then he went running and screaming across the green in pursuit of his enemy, a child.

Michelle and I didn't talk that much after that. We stopped having our flirty smoke breaks together. I saw her now as the sexy racist she was, and she saw me as the sexy decadent leftist that I was. Sometimes I would stare at her, thinking about the beautiful, completely centrist babies we might have had together.

A few weeks later I got a new and better-paid job washing up after the hordes of extras on Mel Gibson's *Braveheart*, which was shooting in the Curragh Camp, and I didn't have to think about any of it any more. 'Thank God,' I remember thinking, 'I won't have to work alongside a crazed racist conspiracy theorist any more. Now I get to work alongside Mel Gibson!'

The shooting of *Braveheart* was a big deal in County Kildare. Mel Gibson and his crew rolled into town and everyone decided to get a piece. The Irish army, who, let's face it, didn't have any wars to be fighting, offered up the Curragh Camp as a base for the crew. And the entirety of the FCA, the Irish reserve army, became kilt-clad, dreadlocked extras for the battle scenes that were to be shot on the Curragh Plains.

I was one of twenty dogsbodies, based in the canteen of the military college, whose job it was to clear away and clean up the dirty dishes soiled by the ravenous FCA men. For this we were being paid the then very substantial sum of two hundred pounds a week. All of us were male, which was probably a product of military sexism, and we were all there as a consequence of nepotism. Ireland in 1994 was a developing nation with notions and the whole of County Kildare was on the take. I saw some people drive home from the film set in the evening with carloads of food. There were rumours of deliveries being redirected to other businesses. I remember an FCA man pointing at an American crew member's watch and saying, 'Can I have that?' *Braveheart* was basically what Kildare got instead of the Marshall Plan.

And the FCA men quickly grew to love Mel Gibson as though he really were Braveheart. This was because, one day before a scene in which his army were meant to moon the enemy, the hated English, Mel demonstrated the act by mooning the entire cast and crew. Yes, they loved him because they had seen his arse. And thus are men bonded to one another.

We dogsbodies did not wear kilts and did not worship Mel. We wore aprons and little paper hats. And everyone had a nickname. These were handed out by a skinny, charismatic young man named Pancho who lived on a run-down estate on the edge of the camp. When Pancho christened you with a nickname it felt like an honour. He'd announce the name dramatically, then he would thoughtfully write it on to your paper hat.

'You're Wurzel,' he said to a young student with a scraggly Wurzel Gummidge-style beard.

'You're Two Foot,' he said to the youngest and shortest member of the group. He later discovered the boy's older brother was among the FCA extras and christened him 'Three Foot.'

He named me 'Junkie' because I was pale and thin and long-haired and, thanks to the very early starts in the morning, I was half asleep most of the time. I thought this was a really cool nickname and hoped it would stick. Seriously, that's the kind of person I was then.

The starts were very early, so although most of us lived very nearby we had the option of being billeted in rows of bunks inside the old red-brick barracks. Because I was young and feckless, I often ended up staying there even when it wasn't necessary. I usually slept in my clothes. But that was fine because it was 1994 and nobody had regular showers then (don't fact-check this).

The Curragh Camp is basically a nineteenth-century British army camp, with barracks accommodation that looks like what you'd see in war films – old red-brick Victorian buildings accessed by external metal stairs and fronted by long metal landings. There was a certain romance to it all, I felt.

Indeed, the first night I was there, my upstairs bunkmate woke in the middle of the night to engage in some rigorous self-love. This was quickly established as a nightly pattern. I became overly familiar with his rhythms and lay taking mental notes in the dark like a teenage Dian Fossey.

'Ah, he's about to finish,' I'd think as I lay there watching the springs go up and down, or

'He's switching things up tonight. Interesting.'

While the wanking was clearly great, the work hours were very long. To compensate, we would make use of the subsidized NCO messes in the camp and drink as much as we could. One early morning after arriving home from a club an hour before our shift started, I watched Pancho vomit all over a rack of just-cleaned dishes.

'Oh, Pancho!' I said, patting him on the back. 'What are you like?' I took each plate, rinsed it lightly with cold water and put it back on the tray.

I saw myself as relatively responsible, but I was not one of life's natural leaders. A stocky young man that Pancho had christened Sarge was the best at talking to our bosses and so became our unofficial foreman. He was a stone-cold psychopath. He could say, 'Yes, sir, we'll get right to that,' in a manner that inspired so much confidence in the listener that even when we did not 'get right to that', all our managers would remember was the way he had made them feel in their hearts.

I remember one day returning from a shoot, four of us rattling along in the back of a big military truck filled with supplies, when Sarge took a fit and began screaming and throwing cups and plates out on the road behind us. I'd never seen anyone go mental before. It was amazing.

'Sarge,' said our manager, who had been driving in a car a little behind us on the road. 'I couldn't help notice that there was loads and loads of broken crockery on the road as I drove to the camp.'

'I noticed that too,' said Sarge. 'What do you think it could be from?'

'Oh, Sarge,' said our manager, chucking him on the chin. In every organization I have worked for since, there has been someone like Sarge.

We dishwashers got to know each other quite well, but we were all very different. While some of us were cosseted children of the officer classes, due to soon return to college courses in the cities, others would be going back to life in minimum-wage jobs or on the dole. One boy got upset one day because he realized for the first time how few opportunities he had. One boy played guitar really well and sang songs for us. One boy had lost his mother and was remarkably open and self-aware about how it had affected him. One boy could talk for hours about Jungianism and Tarot and new-age mysticism. One boy wanked at nights for an average of ten minutes. I could set my watch to it.

At the end of the summer the Americans went away and so did the FCA men and the dogsbodies. The army stayed put. I met one of my co-workers once the following year, but I haven't met any of them since then. That's foreign direct investment for you. In fact, the only one of them I've kept in any sort of contact with is Mel Gibson. He's doing really well. Thanks for asking.

Gravity Blues

When I was nineteen years old, in the summer of 1994, my friends and family all gathered at a field near Naas to watch me die.

They had a picnic. They brought the kids. They all seemed pretty happy about it. They cheered when I appeared on the field. They raised drinks to me. 'When I'm dead you'll feel very silly about this,' I remember thinking, in my flappy white jumpsuit, the costume for the cult I had apparently just joined.

I don't know why I decided to do a parachute jump. It's very out of character for me. It was for charity, but I can't even remember what the charity was, so the charity was definitely not the point.

As I have mentioned before, my dad was in the Ranger Wing, a branch of the Irish army that was trained to battle insurgents, and therefore he was always ruining television programmes ('Children, that model of gun doesn't hold that amount of ammo: this episode of *The Transformers* is a farce') and he was always jumping out of planes. 'I can't talk now,' I remember him saying once, 'I have to go jump out of a plane.'

When I was younger, I had seen a future for myself in which I, too, jumped out of planes, probably in order to do a head-over-heels somersault and shoot a terrorist in the face, but I don't think I harboured any such notions at this particular point in my life. The height of my ambition, at this time, was to be in an indie band and to learn to smoke cigarettes in a cool fashion and to have strangers question my sexuality. I also said things like 'One man's terrorist is another man's freedom fighter,' which definitely ruled me out of membership of any sort of counter-insurgency outfit. Dad couldn't have got me in if he tried.

I think I was in the canteen in the Curragh Camp on the set of the film *Braveheart*, badly washing grease off an extra's plate with cold water and a diphtheria-soaked rag, when someone offered me the opportunity to jump out of a plane. 'Fair enough,' I said, and signed myself up. Seriously, I have no memory of why I did it. That is the core mystery of this piece. If this were a short story, I'd have to workshop it until my main character had a clear motivation.

What I do remember is that as soon as I wrote my name down, I knew that I would be dead four weeks later, and that if anyone beyond my family and friends knew of me in, say, 2020, it would only be because they had passed the bronze plaque on the spot from which I'd been power-hosed.

You see, I am not an adventurous man. I am a hypochondriacal insomniac. My encounters with death are restricted to temporarily dozing off in the driver's seat of a car (terrifying yet life-affirming) and having a scary lump under my arm. ('That's just an infected hair follicle, you pig,' said my doctor. OK, he only said the first bit. The 'pig' bit was just implied.)

Once I'd signed that sheet of paper, my life became filled

with melancholy and darkness. Drinks with friends were shadowed by the nostalgic regrets of a much older man. (As I reread this, I realize 'drinks with friends' is a misleading phrase because when you read it you probably picture a tavern or a dinner party, when what I really mean you to picture is five teenagers in parkas binge-drinking in a ditch.) As we sat there, in our ditch, swigging on Scrumpy Jack and Dutch Gold, breaking off only so some of us could vomit, I would cast my eyes across the faces of my youthful companions and say gnomic things about the passage of time and recite passages of poetry I'd learned in college.

In the evenings I would sit at family meals and think about how my sister and brother would miss my fraternal guidance. I would grip my parents' hands and tears would come to my eyes as I contemplated the tragedy of a parent outliving their child. They seemed heartlessly blasé about the whole thing.

For four weeks I stopped making plans. When I thought of the future, I saw a shot of a biplane flying into the sunset followed by an image of my mother weeping while wearing a fetching black veil. Sometimes, when I put the sequence on autoplay in my head, it cut to an image of my father wearing a fetching black veil too. He looked good in it.

On the day of the parachute jump I made my way to an airstrip in Naas, where I met a parachute instructor named Steve and a bunch of other first-time jumpers. Steve had a tanned, stubbled face and he was big and muscular and he was absolutely bet into his jumpsuit. Seriously. He looked like he'd put on a toddler's onesie by mistake.

My fellow jumpers were all identically dressed in white jumpsuits far roomier than Steve's. I instantly started to fit them into archetypes I'd seen in Vietnam movies. I was the naïve college boy whose book learning had not prepared him for this. There was a hapless yokel named Karl who had huge arms and wanted to shake hands with everyone and talk about his small town in Tennessee, I mean Carlow.

'I'm not here to make friends,' I would have said to him, if I'd been able to speak.

There was also a newly engaged couple seeking to have a bonding experience of death. I had problems fitting this pair into my Vietnam movie, to be honest with you. And I don't really remember who else was there. The reality is that I can only really remember what we spent the day doing. We spent most of it being told all the different ways in which we might die or cripple ourselves. Most of the training was about how to fall in a way that didn't cause us to get sucked into the path of the plane, the sequence to follow if the parachute didn't open at all, and then, if that wasn't enough to worry about, the correct way to land without breaking our legs.

Nowadays, when a first-timer does a parachute jump, they do so strapped to the front of an instructor in a harness much like the type of harness a baby might be carried around in.

In those days, however, the parachutes for first-timers had a line connecting the parachute ripcord to the plane. Then, when they plummeted screaming from the plane, this line automatically pulled the ripcord, and the chute was deployed without the first-timer having to do anything.

This was, as Steve kept reminding us, the way things

would play out if everything went well. If all did not go well and we weren't killed instantly by the propellers of the plane (he knew someone this had happened to), we might instead find ourselves plummeting with a malfunctioning parachute and would have a matter of seconds during which we would have to a) discard the unopened chute and b) deploy the extra emergency chute, all by ourselves.

Oh, and if we deployed the emergency chute when the other chute was already open, both chutes could become entangled and we would fall to our deaths (he also knew of someone this had happened to).

And then we would have to check the direction the runway flags were blowing in order to manoeuvre into the wind, thus reducing our speed, and crash-land into the ground at a speed that was still violent enough to kill us (he knew of someone this had happened to).

And we had to avoid power lines so as not to fly into them and electrocute ourselves to death. (Yes. Steve knew someone this had happened to. His address book was apparently filled with crossed-out names and 'RIP' etched in biro beside them.)

The whole thing was the kind of exercise in pessimism that is rejected nowadays by advocates of positive thinking. 'Planning for failure is the behaviour of a failure,' a self-help guru once told me. He had clearly never done parachute training with Steve.

If I had been the kind of person who expressed emotion when bad things happened to me, I would have spent the entire duration of our training sobbing, screaming and rending my garments and hair. Instead I did what I always do during the worst moments of my life: I went through the motions filled with dread, my mouth open like a slack-jawed fool's. Any words, when they came, were monosyllabic and a little bit slurred. The word I used was usually 'what?'

Would you like to break for coffee? 'What?'

Are you OK? 'What?'

How many fingers am I holding up? 'What?'

Karl the yokel, on the other hand, was chatty throughout.

'Agh, me legs!' he cried as we practised our landings. 'I've busted my legs! Find me a sexy nurse!'

'Oh no, my chute didn't open!' he said as we practised the emergency sequence. 'Collect my body parts and find me a sexy nurse!'

'Bombs away!' he said as we practised leaping from a model of the plane doorway on to the grass. 'Find me a sexy nurse!'

I did not want Karl's to be the last voice I heard before I died. I could see Steve had similar thoughts. I imagine that he spent a lot of time considering whether to give Karl 'the bad parachute'. Now this is pure supposition on my part, but I reckon every parachute club has a 'bad parachute' stashed away just in case the need arises. I mean, what if a terrorist hijacks the plane, or the taxman visits, or someone like Karl turns up and starts being a total dose?

As the day wore on, I had less, not more, confidence about whether I would still be alive come sunset. My family and friends and neighbours arrived out on to the airstrip under the illusion that it was a happy occasion. My dad was filming it all for some reason, and in the video I look several shades paler than I usually am.

In the film you can see me thinking: 'What are you doing filming this? This is going to be a goddamn snuff film, you monster. *Why don't you stop me? Jesus Christ, what are you all just standing around for? Save me, you bastards!*' Of course, social embarrassment stopped me from saying this and instead, in the video, I can be seen drinking red lemonade and pretending to be interested in something my friend Corncrake is saying.

And then it was time to board the plane. It was tiny. It was even smaller than I expected it to be. There was room for a pilot and then room for me, Steve, Karl and half of the recently engaged couple. I can't remember which half.

Steve, sitting upfront to oversee us as we were dispatched, hooked all of our chutes to the plane and grinned evilly. Karl was beside him. I was behind Karl and behind me was the third person, who, in my memory, is just a beige oval face above a white jumpsuit. We had to sit hunched up on our knees. The door of the plane was open the whole time and it was almost impossible to hear anything over the buzz of the plane's engines. When we reached a height of, I think, five thousand feet, Steve turned to us and shouted: 'Right, it's time to jump.'

I knew at that moment that I would not be able to do so, because it was completely insane, and I decided I would tell Steve this. But Karl was ahead of me and I also decided, out of politeness, to wait until he killed himself first.

So, while we're waiting for my turn, let me tell you how you jump from a small plane:

First you reach out of the plane, above the tremendous void of air that falls for thousands of feet beneath you, and you grab, with your right hand, the beam that runs diagonally from the base of the plane up to the wing.

Then you step on to the step below the door, your right hand still grasping the beam, and grab another bit of the beam with your other hand.

Then, despite millions of years of evolution during which we did not grow wings, you step off of the aforementioned step and hang by the arms from the beam, your legs flapping in the air, very, very high above your mortal enemy, the ground.

Then Steve counts to three and, if you're Karl, you do not let go and you continue to hang there with a panicked expression on your face.

'Let go!' said Steve.

'I've changed my mind,' said Karl.

No. That's wrong. I'm getting the tone wrong. Let me try again. It was more like:

'I've changed my mind,' screamed Karl, screamingly, from his screaming face.

'You can't change your mind,' said Steve.

'I want to get back in,' screamed Karl, hanging from the wing of a plane five thousand feet above the ground.

'I can't let you back in,' said Steve. 'It's too dangerous.'

'*Aaaaagh*,' said Karl.

'Sorry, Karl, I can't let you back in,' said Steve firmly, as though talking to a toddler, a toddler whom he was forcing to jump from a plane.

'*Aaaaaagh,*' said Karl.

Here's something important I learned from my time with Karl: there is only so much time you can spend hanging for dear life to the wing of a plane before you lose strength and have to let go. In Karl's case, it was around two minutes. Then he lost his grip and plunged to what to him must have seemed like imminent death but was really just a sensation of imminent death that humans flirt with because we have no natural predators and have evolved into something ridiculous.

I mean, seriously, when they invented the parachute, it was a pragmatic safety device. It was not planned for danger aficionados like Steve or weekend adventurers like Karl or obsessive neurotics like me or vague oval blobs like the person sitting behind me. What's wrong with us?

Anyway, that exchange between Steve in the plane and Karl hanging from the wing of the plane is still the most interesting conversation I have ever witnessed. I've not seen nor heard anything like it to this day – and I've done acid. Then as Karl fell to his possible death, Steve turned to me, calm as you like, and said: 'Your turn.'

At that point I realized something important about myself. I realized that I would rather die screaming than be a little bit embarrassed in front of a hunky stranger. So, I grabbed the beam with my right hand, stood on the step overlooking the void, clung to the wing for dear life, listened to Steve count to three, and then I let go. 'I might be about to die,' I thought. 'But I'm better than you, Kaaaaaaarl.'

What I actually said was '*Aaaaaaagh.*'

I spiralled about in the air for a while in a manner Steve had tried to teach us not to do, before feeling the sensation of being yanked upward into the air, as though some big celestial fingers had grabbed me by the scruff of the neck. I felt certain, at that point, that my parachute had become caught in the propellers of the plane. In fact, and this shouldn't come as a surprise to you, unless you assumed this essay was found on my corpse and hastily written as I plummeted to my death, it was just the sensation of my chute deploying and my earthward velocity diminishing.

And then it dawned on me that I wasn't going to die. I was euphoric. Here's an actual thought I had: 'The worst that's going to happen to me now is that I will shatter my legs on landing!' And then I shouted, 'Woohoo!' and I screamed with joy, and I thought, 'I'm going to do this again! Over and over again! I'm going to become a parachute guy. Paddy Parachute, they'll call me. I'll move in with Steve and become a local character. I'll wear this jumpsuit for ever and always have a parachute on my back, "just in case"! That will be my thing now.'

I could see Karl's dejected-looking parachute below me. Ha! Karl had been made to look like a prize fool. Not me. I was a golden god of the skies, lord of all I surveyed. I had only screamed a little bit. I could see the county spread out below me – birds in flight, livestock, hills and plains and drumlins, my stupid family. Several weeks of ominous foreboding evaporated into a glorious rush of life. I was nineteen years old. My whole future lay ahead of me and I got to look down upon creation and mock it.

It doesn't look quite as cool on film. My father isn't the world's best cinematographer, and the video gives the impression that I landed on top of a sheep. For the record: I didn't land on top of a sheep. It's an optical illusion created by my father's inability to correctly follow my downward trajectory behind an unfortunately placed hillock.

As soon as I had landed, any thought I had of going parachuting again instantly vanished. I was over it as soon as I touched the ground. Steve, who was clearly eager to become a cautionary tale in another instructor's training banter, instantly offered me the opportunity to go back up again.

'Fuck you, Steve,' I said.

OK, I didn't say that. I said: 'You're grand, thanks, Steve.' The point was the same, however: Steve and his parachutes meant nothing to me now.

I went back to my normal life, collecting and washing plates for FCA men in kilts who were in thrall to a rage-filled Australian. I never did anything like jump from a plane ever again. I don't know why I did it in the first place. I genuinely don't. Nowadays, if I want to flirt with death, I just find a strange lump to obsess about or read the Twitter feed of the American president. I can feel death's presence everywhere now.

Talking to Strangers

(My life as a journalist)

A colleague once spent a long time trying to put together a piece about people affected by a particularly tragic scenario. She was finding it hard to locate interviewees who were willing to talk. One day she came into the office and told me that she had finally, through hard work, found another instance of this terrible circumstance. So we high-fived.

'Are we bad people?' I thought, almost instantly.

I worry about this all the time.

1

My job is to strip-mine conversations for incident and detail, and then create a story with what I've found out. The idea is that there is edification and interest and entertainment in the story that I write and that you will figure that it's worth paying money to read it and other things like it.

The job frequently involves approaching complete strangers and talking to them. Approaching a stranger in public always feels like a deeply unnatural thing to do. Each and every time I do it, I feel as though I have to break a part of my brain. It never really gets any easier or feels normal. I have spent days approaching strangers on public transport, in bars, libraries, taxi ranks, homeless shelters and busy streets. Before I approach a stranger in one of these places, my feet feel fused to the ground. There is a flutter in my chest and the beginnings of a headache. Luckily, my fear of approaching people I don't know is outmatched by my fear of not meeting my deadlines. So, usually, after about twenty minutes of hesitation, I lurch into somebody's path and say:

'I'm sorry for disturbing you, I'm a journalist with the *Irish Times* and . . .'

At this point, anything can happen. Some people don't even hear what I'm saying and assume that I'm either begging or trying to sell them something. 'No, thank you,' they say, and wave their hands at me. '*I am not begging!*' I once called after a businessman in a nice suit who facepalmed me.

But most people will stop to talk. They have things to say, or, more usually, they just want to help and, as they try to help, they realize they have something to say.

Here are some things I've learned:

1) For all the much-vaunted distrust of the press that's out there, people are still touchingly eager to talk to me. I guess usually nobody's listening.

2) The easiest scenario in which to start a conversation is when the person is in the act of doing something. What they are doing can be familiar or strange: it doesn't matter, it's an opening. This means that I regularly find myself drawn to situations that other people instinctively recoil from – two teenagers sifting through their own vomit with a lollypop

stick, for example (they were looking for drugs they had swallowed to hide from the guards). 'What are you doing?' is an excellent ice-breaker. People love to tell you what they are doing.

3) People don't know the most interesting things about their own life stories. Their more intriguing anecdotes usually come as asides and afterthoughts. So after ten minutes talking to a gentle, apparently homeless man covered with pigeons in Stephen's Green, he tells me, 'Of course, that was when I was working for a German investment bank.' Or after a long conversation with a youth activist, during which he has insisted that his story of being taken into care at the age of four isn't that interesting, he says: 'So I'd barricaded myself into Mam's bedroom with all the knives.'

4) In real life, there are no stock characters. I once met a journalist who told me that he fabricated some of his 'man on the street' interviews. Apart from being ethically appalled by this, I couldn't understand it. Much as I hate approaching strangers on the street, it's also the best part of my job. People regularly say things to me that, if put in the mouth of a fictional character, you'd think were implausibly erudite or insightful or weird or eccentric or beautiful. I'm not good enough at fiction to better it. Neither was the fraudulent journalist. His vox-pops spoke like characters from a bad soap opera.

2

Prearranged interviews with famous people are another weird kind of conversation. They're very different from the conversations I have with random people I meet in public places. Before these interviews with famous people I spend hours drafting and redrafting lists of questions in a little black notebook. Can you imagine having a conversation with someone who has thoroughly researched you and has mapped out their conversational topics in a notebook? Maybe you can. Maybe, in a networked world, that's normal now. Maybe that's what dating with Tinder is like.

One way or another, soon the list in my notebook looks like the jottings on a conspiracy theorist's wall. There are under-linings, arrows, marginal scrawls, circlings and crossing-outs. It eventually becomes illegible so I find a new page and write the list up again, in a new and better order.

The order of the questions is very important. I consider different scenarios that might play out when I'm having the conversation. I consider the things that I'm sure the famous person will want to talk about. I consider what I know about the subject's personality, whether they are euphemistically described by others as 'difficult' and whether that has any basis in fact. I have, in particular, considered the timing and placement of the more controversial questions, the ones they possibly hope I will not ask and the ones I hope they'll bring up unprompted (they sometimes do bring these things up unprompted). In my brain I will have worked out a few scenarios in which those more difficult questions can emerge in a way that looks organic and natural.

By the time we meet, I've been looking at that list all morning, so I don't need to look at it while we talk. Instead I spend the whole meeting looking directly at the famous person in a way that would unnerve a less famous person. We're pleased to see each other. They want me to like them. That's why even slightly public people are public people. I also want them to like me.

And then, over the course of the conversation, we start to bond. This is a very real, very human and completely superficial bond. The famous person might not even remember me the next time we meet. This bond is what happens when any two humans speak to one another for over an hour. You can sometimes have the same experience chatting with a stranger on a long train journey.

The conversations follow a rough pattern. At the beginning, the interviewee might have an agenda that they want to lay out for me, about the thing they are promoting or the initiative they are spearheading. It's when they've exhausted *that* material that things get interesting, because outside of psychotherapy people do not normally get to talk all about themselves uninterrupted for an hour. Their defences drop.

This happens at around the twenty-five-minute mark. By that point, we've warmed to each other and they start to surprise themselves with the things they're telling me and the things they remember about themselves. Sometimes I watch people actively forgetting that they're doing an interview. Seriously, sometimes people will reveal something private just to fill a gap in the conversation.

I'm not interested in gotcha moments or scandalous details or compulsively clickable news headlines (apologies to any of my editors who wish I was). In some ways I am a terrible, terrible journalist. What I want is to feast on the rich, rich detail that makes up a person's life – the spontaneous turns of phrase, the newly recalled biographical matter, the latter-day insights, their own emotional engagement with the material of their existence. I want all that good old life mulch! I am an information vampire. I should probably be in jail.

3

Here's how I dress when I'm out doing a general reporting job: dark corduroys (denim looks weird on my legs), a plain yellow/green anorak, scuffed blue and white runners (bought for running but not used for running) and a small brown backpack.

There are practical reasons for having a get-up like this in a rainy country, but the clothes are also important because they don't say much about who I am. They're neutral. I've found that it's easier to get people talking if they aren't burdened by preconceived notions about me. That doesn't happen so easily if I am, for example, wearing a V-neck jumper and a peacoat and Doc Martens and look like the ageing hipster/*Irish Times* journalist that I actually am.

And yes, this is one of those admissions that make me worry. To be clear, I didn't start dressing like this as a conscious form of manipulation. I just noticed that I was doing it and I sort of interviewed myself about it. *This* is the type of information that comes out at the twenty-five-minute mark when I'm being honest with myself.

4

I have transcribed thousands of hours of interview tapes. I usually transcribe every word of every interview. This is the worst part of my job, but it feels like some kind of offering in return for all the things that have been disclosed to me. I also learn things from transcription. Here are some of the things that I have learned from hours spent transcribing things:

1) Most people, except a handful of ridiculously eloquent conversational savants, do not actually speak in the way that you think they do when you hear them. Our brains edit out the majority of false starts and redundancies and hesitations and *ums* and *aws* well before they ever reach our consciousness. Many people, myself included, are incapable of finishing a sentence, and you only realize the extent of this when you've recorded someone and are attempting to transcribe what they've said. I, like you, have held forth at a dinner

table, certain that I was soliloquizing like a wartime prime minister or Shakespearean hero. Deep down, I know the truth: as a species, we're barely verbal and I am grunting like a baboon.

2) You know the way people say they can't stand the sound of their voice on tape because it sounds so different from the way it sounds in their head? Not me. I sound the same to myself in my head as I do on tape. I know this wasn't always the case: I remember once being shocked and surprised at how I sounded. But I've been listening to my own voice for so long now that I've rewritten my own brain chemistry on the subject and I hear myself when I speak now in the same way that I sound on tape. I literally like the sound of my own voice. Is that such a terrible admission to make? Yes. Yes, it is.

3) There is a range of narrative possibilities with every interview. An hour-long conversation with a fast speaker can lead to a typed transcription that's nine thousand words long. Completists might say, 'I'd like to read all of it.' They'd be desperately bored. The subject might confess to murder at the fortieth minute, but you won't read that far: you'd have zoned out by minute fifteen, when he's recounting the best way to fill a dishwasher. Journalists try to pick the things from the transcript that will be most enlightening or useful for the readers. This is where some PR people get

fierce confused. They often assume we will select
the stuff that makes the subject look cool.
Occasionally, we get strange phone calls
afterwards and we have to remind the PR person
that we don't actually work for them. Like I said,
people don't always appreciate the interesting bits
of their own story. They would look at the same
nine-thousand-word transcript and create a totally
different narrative. So would a different
journalist. So would you.

4) Charisma is a terrible thing. This has been my
most startling discovery. I have occasionally left
the company of musically voiced, theatrically
limbed glad-handers in no doubt that I have just
done the interview of my career, only to find
myself later transcribing dead words on the page.
Like weird sea creatures who can mimic more
impressive species, some humans have learned to
ape the contours and emphases of an interesting
conversation without actually saying anything
interesting. A large proportion of them are CEOs
and politicians. Some of them are writers.

I have also concluded apparently lifeless interviews
with plodding bores, only to find that what they were
actually saying, when I typed it up, was absolutely
fascinating.

Charisma is a magic trick and my guard goes up
when people have it. I try to listen harder to the
people who don't.

5

Sometimes when talking to a stranger, it's hard not to find yourself being deeply moved. I have sat and listened to the saddest stories told to me by people who didn't deserve to have sad things happen to them. On a few occasions I've come close to bursting into tears. For the most part I've learned how to hide it. Journalists are meant to have the straight-faced demeanour of a doctor or a therapist.

I once sat in the office of the activist priest Peter McVerry as he told me how he began providing services to homeless people. While we were talking, his little dog, Jack, growled at me with justified suspicion. Then a very skinny, very dirty young man shuffled into the room and just sat quietly in the chair beside me, his head bowed. Father McVerry kept talking and, as he did so, I noticed that his little dog, so dubious about me, was licking the young man's hands. It was too much for me, I don't know why, and my eyes started to fill with tears. I put my hands over my face and I hoped nobody noticed.

(On the same visit, another young man saw my long hair and beard and greeted me with the cheerful phrase: 'How-iya, Fat Jesus.')

6

One day I got a phone call at the office. It was a man I had met a few months before while visiting a drop-in service for homeless people. He had been friendly and incisive. He had once been a jockey. He had sad, red-rimmed eyes.

'I have a story for you,' he said over the phone. 'On Saturday I'm going to kill myself to draw attention to homelessness.'

My heart felt as though it had stopped in my chest. He was giving me this scoop, he said, because he liked me. Because I had listened to him and he felt like I cared, and so few people he had met seemed to care.

'Please don't do that,' I said.

I told him that we couldn't cover a story like that and I told him that I was worried about him and that I wanted to know where he was. He didn't want to hear any of this. He proceeded to tell me more about what he planned to do. I gathered that he was in a different city now (his thing was moving around; he couldn't stay put) and as he outlined his plan to kill himself, I discovered exactly where he was.

I asked could I call him back. My observant colleague Emma had heard my panic and had already found me the numbers for people in homeless services in the city where he was staying and the local branch of the Samaritans. I spent most of the day calling different NGOs and social workers while also talking regularly with this sad-voiced man.

I could only sleep when, a few days later, it was clear that social services were in contact with him and I was assured, over the phone, that he was not actually going to kill himself.

I've also interviewed volunteers with the Samaritans.

They told me stark, beautifully matter-of-fact stories about talking to suicidal people, people who were, as they talked, walking through the woods to find a place to die or lying in bed after swallowing a blister-pack of pills. They told me that sometimes, after an hour of such talk, the person resolved to wait another day, thanked them and then went away to make a cup of tea or call an ambulance. Sometimes, they said, the line just went dead, and they never found out what happened.

7

Here's what my life looks like when I'm out on the road. I start with a fretful, coffee-fuelled early-morning drive (now I get a Pavlovian jolt of pleasure just passing motorway service stations). When I reach my destination, I try to negotiate the parking logistics and then find the busiest street and start talking to people. If I'm doing my job well, I've arranged some tent-pole interviews with public figures to be met over the course of the day but, for the most part, I'm talking to complete strangers and I'm approaching them unheralded.

If I'm on a daily deadline, I scribble notes as I go and run into quiet corners and coffee shops every two hours or so to type them up. Early in the day, filled with dread, I might ring the office suggesting that things aren't going too well. I might ask for a shorter wordcount than that requested. My editors may or may not say, 'Fine.' I always feel that the article I have to write is on the cusp of failure.

Then I speak to loads and loads of strangers. At a certain point I realize that I'm enjoying myself. At around three I might contact the office again to ask for extra space because I was totally wrong earlier and I have loads of material and people are endlessly fascinating and say the most unexpected things. I like them. I like people. I sometimes forget that.

At around four or five I retreat to some place that offers coffee and broadband and I try to throw everything into some kind of narrative in time to be filed by seven o'clock. At this point I feel very exhilarated and very alone.

8

Some people have been waiting their whole life for a journalist to talk to them. I've met several vulnerable people who carry plastic bags filled with documentation – birth certs, official letters, news clippings. They have a story and they are certain that this documentation tells that story. It often does not. My heart goes out to them. Everyone does have a story. It's just not always one they're able to tell, and it's not always the one they think they have.

Not everyone wants to talk to me.

I once went into a small shop in a small Welsh town. It had narrow aisles and shelves rammed with bargain kitchen towels and porcelain cats and clown figurines. Behind the counter sat a man with straggly, long grey hair, sallow skin and bags under his eyes. I thought, because this is how I think, 'He'll be interesting.'

He *was* interesting. After I introduced myself, he jumped up from his seat and started to shout, with a quiver in his voice: 'You must go. You must go.'

I assumed he'd misunderstood something. So, I started to explain again. 'No,' I said. 'I'm a journalist. I'm writing a piece for the newspaper about . . .'

He started shouting, into my face. '*You are dangerous. You are dangerous people.*'

He spoke like that, loudly and without contractions. He was a lot shorter than me, but he was strong. He put one hand on my shoulder and the other on my elbow and he started to forcibly steer me through the grimacing porcelain statuettes, out to the street. '*You are dangerous people.*'

'I don't understand,' I said.

'*Stop talking to me,*' he said, and when we got outside, he actually put his hands over his ears as though my words might hurt him.

The street was busy and people were staring. I was now standing in front of the shop and the man was standing framed in the doorway with his hands on his ears and his shoulders hunched as though I was about to hit him.

'I'm not doing anything,' I said, more for the benefit of onlookers than for him, because he clearly couldn't hear me any more.

Every time I opened my mouth he spoke over me. '*You are frightening me!*' he shouted, and he said this without making eye contact. '*I will call the police on you, I am very frightened.*'

9

I worry a lot about how to represent people fairly – not the politicians and celebrities who are well used to talking with people like me, but the people who never expected a journalist to turn up in their lives.

I worry about misquoting people and I go back endlessly to check my Dictaphone recordings and ring people up to clarify that what I understood them to mean is what they actually meant. I worry about getting things wrong. I worry about accidentally making people look bad or that I will unintentionally embarrass them.

I worry about whether my duty is to the interviewee or to my readers, and I know that the truth is that I have a responsibility to both. It can be hard to find the right balance. I mean, should I include the slightly bigoted thing the man said after he talked about his father dying? Is it fair to include an unintentionally controversial line the actor uttered that will overshadow the rest of a thoughtful interview?

I've always heard the term 'emotional intelligence' presented as a positive, but I've come to understand it as a morally neutral thing. Emotional intelligence allows you to read a room. What you do with that knowledge once you have it is up to you and it's not something to take lightly.

In a way, I might be a better journalist if I was a little more psychopathic. My empathy can go a little haywire. Put me at the Eurovision or a concert by Daniel O'Donnell or a gathering of conspiracy theorists and all of my snark disappears and I see it all through the eyes of the people who love being there.

For life-long caregivers of disabled relatives, watching Daniel O'Donnell do a ridiculous broom dance is an oasis of joy.

For the conspiracy theorist who feels buffeted by the vagaries of an uncertain existence, the crazy master narrative provides a needed sense of control.

For two star-crossed lovers who met in Belfast's only gay bar in the 1980s, the Eurovision is a utopian respite from sectarianism and homophobia. Silly love songs can save people's lives.

There are problems with this tendency of mine to fit in. I am not the person you'd get to write a takedown of even the most despicable person. I would be likely to meet the subject, find them surprisingly charming, and end up praising their idiosyncratic worldview and noting how they graciously paid for my coffee.

10

One winter's day on Dame Street I was with an *Irish Times* photographer named Dara, trailing the street team of a homelessness charity, when they stopped to give a sandwich and a cup of tea to a very friendly, slightly drunk man whom they knew very well.

The man had chapped lips and broken capillaries on his

face, but he was all warmth and good humour. As we spoke, another man stopped to talk to him. It was a social worker from the shelter where the homeless man's girlfriend lived. Everyone was looking for him, the social worker said, because his mother was dead.

The homeless man collapsed into himself. He started to cry. He wondered aloud if it could be true. He didn't believe it was true. He talked to us about his mother and his impossibly large family and when they had last seen one another. The people from the homelessness charity contacted someone to come and collect him and bring him to where his girlfriend was, but before his lift arrived, the people from the charity had to move on. There were other people who needed sleeping bags and hot drinks and food.

We followed the people from the charity, but after a hundred yards Dara, the photographer, stopped and swore. Then he said, 'We can't leave him like that.' I looked back. The man was standing in the middle of the pre-Christmas crowd, drunk, newly bereaved, numb and alone.

'I'm going back to wait with him,' said Dara. And he went back. He didn't think this man, who had just lost his mother, should be left on his own.

He took no photographs for the rest of the night. Instead, he waited with the man until the car came to collect him. When the piece came out, because, oh, you'd better believe it, I wrote that piece, it was accompanied by photographs taken on another day by another photographer. Dara did the human thing. He stayed. I think about this all the time.

Sing a New Song to Drive Sorrows Away

Every winter my wife and I go to a windswept coastal town in Northumberland to sing folk songs, guided by a famous English folk family. We've been doing this for eight years. When we get there we drink real ale and eat well and learn how to sing harmonies on top of old songs about shipwrecks and selkies and people being pressganged to fight in foreign wars.

We are, it's true, revelling in ancient misery while eating pies, but the music has a huge effect on me. When I am singing in a large group, I can hear frail voices getting stronger and strong voices getting gentler and, slowly, I feel the edges of everyone disappearing until we have blended into one entity. It's terrifying and it's beautiful. I simultaneously feel very present and as though I might disappear. And when that happens I feel tears in my eyes, and a crack in my voice reminds me of my own individuality for a moment. It's not just that my voice blends with the others but it feels like my self does too. And I start to cry.

I once read somewhere that music preceded language. Mothers sang to bond themselves to their children and then some ambitious leader thought to sing to bond himself to his tribe and it was only later that language began to attach itself to that melodic sense of belonging. I don't know if this is true, but it *feels* true.

This is why we have national anthems. That's why tribal leaders and bards would sing, not speak, the story of their tribe. This is why people sang rebel songs and union songs and hymns, because when we are in harmony we are blissfully in thrall to the group. These songs have a purpose. They're there to keep time (fall out of rhythm in a sea shanty and you might lose a finger). They're there to unite the working man against his capitalist oppressor. They're there to remind us of love of country or the danger of the sea or the tragedies that come with loving an outsider. They're there to bond us together.

I can feel that bond when I sing with other people, and if you were to randomly throw in some malign ideology on top of that sense of melodic belonging, I'd probably subscribe to it. If you were to subtly introduce a nefarious manifesto into the lyrics just as a minor harmony descended, I'd be yours. I'd be out with you on the front lines, flinging Molotov cocktails at the children of the enemy with all the other true believers.

Such messaging is unlikely up in Northumberland. Most of the people I sing with there are members of the bohemian bourgeoisie – teachers, social workers, left-leaning vicars, carpenters, retired academics. The most terrifying dogma I might subscribe to with this lot is an overwhelming desire to hear someone out.

So, every year I go there to sing and to lose myself. It's the only thing that works. When we learn a song, there's a period during which each run-through requires thought and concentration and nothing sounds quite right. But then, slowly, we approach a moment when the music becomes effortless and the lines intertwine into those huge human chords and I find myself completely undone. I feel a powerful surge of emotion. I feel moved. I feel sad and happy at the same time and I simply don't know what to do with myself but keep singing, even though I'm often singing while trying not to cry.

I have no idea where this feeling was all the rest of my life.

Everyone's voice is different. There are fat voices and thin voices. Strong voices and weak voices. High voices and low voices. Smooth voices that hit a pure note, and rough voices, ragged with texture and harmonics and lives lived to the full. There were also, I once believed, good voices and bad voices. My dad had a good voice. My mother, we were told, did not. Her older sister and her brother, both now gone, sang beautifully. She and her surviving sister, Phil, avoided singing at all costs. They didn't have a note in their heads, they said.

The family likes to joke about this. My dad would sing two songs to us when we were small, songs I remember clearly. There was 'The Scottish Soldier', a song about a death-weary warrior that was popularized by the light entertainer Andy Stewart, and 'Danny Boy', an Irish song about separation and loss that was written by an Englishman. My mother also sang songs for us, but we only remember her singing one. This, the family jokes, is because she sings all songs with the same tune. And we all laugh at this, even though it's not entirely fair.

What I don't say is that I loved it when she sang to me. I love those many songs with the one tune, the only tune she sings, because there is something truthful in even the most raggedly sung lines. Everyone's voice is beautiful when they're singing. So nowadays I feel bad for mocking my mother and my aunt. And now they're the only ones in their family left to sing anything.

We weren't a particularly musical family. I wished we were. I would later watch in awe at my friend Barry's house when his family would pass around a guitar and everyone would sing a song. 'People do this?!' I thought.

I already knew there was another, more melodic world out there. I would watch musicals on the telly and dream of scenarios in which I might break into song on the street and passers-by might join in. My first romantic fantasy about a girl involved me and her spontaneously bursting into a duet of 'I Got You Babe'. It was, specifically, the UB40/Chrissie Hynde version, which is, objectively, the best version.

I rehearsed this fantasy over and over in my head. In it, we're both wearing short-sleeved beige leisure suits with belts and excessive pockets and we are up in exotic Dublin, in the Ilac shopping centre with all the other sophisticates. We are about ten, but nobody is wondering where our parents are, because in my fantasy life I resided alone in a flash 1960s apartment like the Thunderbirds lived in. Instead, everyone is stopping to admire our singing and to join in.

Reality was very different. My yearning for a singing-based lifestyle was undercut by the fact that my primary school's choir mistress was one of the most terrifying people I have ever met. Ireland's prohibition of corporal punishment in 1982 was seen by some teachers as a suggestion rather than a rule. They could be cruel. The choir mistress felt that the best way to nurture the singer inside every child was to circle them as they sang, stopping sporadically to shriek with rage. She did this whenever we forgot a line, but in my memory this woman is always shrieking; her hair is wild and her face is contorted; her eyes are different sizes and her mouth is open and her nostrils are flared and her jaw is twisted mid-shriek. I'm pretty sure she didn't look like this all the time. I'm pretty sure she didn't look like that when talking softly to friends, or in her passport photo. But that is, nonetheless, how I remember her.

Her choir was not a meritocracy. She had favourites who tended to be the more tuneful offspring of the professional classes. Favouring the latter was a bit of a tendency in our socioeconomically diverse school. One year when the local doctor and his wife arrived halfway through a nativity play, the principal insisted that the whole thing be performed again from the beginning.

Coming from right in the middle of the class spectrum, I was almost invisible to her, I think. I don't remember ever being praised for my singing during choir practices, but I also don't remember being made to just stand there silently miming, as several of my classmates were instructed to do. I did *not* achieve a sense of harmonic oneness with the universe while singing in this woman's choir. If singing made me cry in those days, it was for the wrong reasons.

When I rediscovered music-making in my mid-teens, it was via garage bands. This is very liberating after you've previously experienced music as a sort of hierarchical terror state. However, singing is not the most important consideration when you form one of these three-chord combos. Singing, in the context of a school garage band, is an afterthought. It comes after you've spent many hours wrangling unholy noise from electric guitars and a badly set-up drum kit.

Here's how a lead singer was chosen in this kind of band: several teenagers gathered in a garage, and if one of them didn't have an instrument, they became the singer. If everyone had an instrument, people opted out of the singing chore one by one, until the person least opposed to the idea became the singer. If more than one person was unopposed to being the singer, then, over time, the person who could bellow most forcibly got the job, because the drummer was always too loud in a garage band and the PA system was always too weak. If anyone actively *wanted* to sing, they had suspiciously healthy self-esteem for Ireland in the 1980s/90s and they were probably not in your friend group to begin with.

And so I became a singer in bands through a combination of other people's lack of interest and the attrition of frailer vocal cords. Being the best singer didn't come into it. This is not unique in musical history. When music was a mnemonic device, the bards weren't the most melodic singers, they were the people with the best memories. The men who led the work songs in chain gangs and on plantations were those with the best sense of rhythm. And similarly, the singers of loud Irish bands in the 1990s were those who could survive a bad PA system.

The way I learned to sing was by aping the singers I loved, regionally inappropriate accents and all. Many of these singers had voices that were charismatically interesting rather than straightforwardly beautiful. My role models were people like Nick Cave, an Australian who sang like a southern US preacher, and Shane McGowan, a Londoner who sang like a member of The Dubliners.

I now recognize that there's a beauty to these voices, but back then I was attracted to them because of the empowering sense they gave me that they were getting away with something. Boys aren't expected or encouraged to have beautiful voices, no more than they are expected or encouraged to have beautiful faces.

I never really thought about my voice then. What it sounded like. What its range was. Whether it was strong or weak. I just sang. And the small rock venues of Ireland actively work against beautification. You spend your time, instead, yearning for audibility and finding tricks to cut through reverberant rooms and bad PA systems and the apathy of shell-shocked sound engineers who have heard too much. My band was also in thrall to a very liberating DIY punk ethic that showcased lo-fi recording techniques and rudimentary skillsets, and if ever we seemed in danger of producing something too pretty, some members of our entourage began to look worried.

It was only when I formed a country band with my friend Anna that I realized that maybe I could aim for beauty with singing. I learned that there was a name for my type of voice – that I was a baritone. I learned that you could choose keys to suit your range and not just stick to the ones your band knew. It was the first time I sang in harmony. I began to appreciate how to sing effectively with other people. There's a way in which you can alter the timbre of your voice to blend in with the person who's telling the story in a way that makes *them* sound better. Alternatively, you can glissando up and down the scale loudly in a way that says, '*And I am also here*' and actively undermine your singing partner. That can be fun too, to be honest.

Anna, with whom I formed that country band, is now my wife. It was like a real-life version of my youthful Ilac centre fantasy. She bewitched me with song like the sirens of yore, like Chrissie Hynde bewitched UB40. In the early days, our relationship felt indistinguishable from the music that we sang together. The voices blended and so did the people. Duet partners often end up together and I am never surprised. It was at this time in my life that singing began to make me cry.

I don't play gigs with a band any more, but I sing more than ever. If anything, it was when I stopped trying to be a professional singer that I really started to enjoy singing. I have sung at weddings, I have sung at christenings and I have sung at too many funerals. I've sung to welcome people and I've sung to say goodbye. Now, whenever I am at a loss or I'm feeling lost, I sing.

I like that the music is now part of my everyday life in a

way that I once craved when I was younger. Anna is melodically prolific. She projectile-sings melodies all over the place. She sings about our cat. She sings about local animals she has seen. And she sings about our nephews, the loons. I add harmonies to these spontaneous renderings, largely so that when she is eventually committed, the orderlies will take me with her. I wouldn't last five minutes doing fifths in an empty kitchen on my own.

We have started to organize singing nights in our home and in the homes of friends. We pick a song, sit around an instrument and have a go.

I don't know why singing makes me cry. But I think it's because when we construct a song from the air with our memories and lungs and mouths, I feel connected to other people in a way I struggle with otherwise. I like losing myself in the thickets of other people's voices, in my friends' voices. We're people in middle age and life has happened to us: bereavement, separation, children, no children, ill health, redundancy, pain. Sometimes you can hear it in the way we sing.

In the folk community, songs from the past are collected reverently like precious treasure; but to lose yourself in harmony you don't really need a sacred relic. You can sing ABBA. You can sing Take That. You can sing an advertising jingle. All you need for that harmonic good stuff to start fizzing around your nervous system is a scrap of melody and some other people. In a sense, all tunes are old tunes that retool the same melodic phrases over and over (apologies here to copyright lawyers). It's all folk music. We're all folk.

The Story of My Brother's Birth, Starring Me

The day my brother was born, I broke my wrist and got a lot of attention and then he went missing. It was quite a day.

My brother is still annoyed about me breaking my arm. 'Even on the day of my birth you stole the limelight,' he says, in what, if you knew him, you'd know to be his customary whining manner.

'I didn't do it on purpose!' I say, crossing my fingers behind my back.

I assume I didn't do it on purpose. But to be honest with you, I have no idea what my thought process was at the time. I was a different man then – I was seven years old – and there were a lot of haphazard elements circulating the origins of my brother. He was what, in those days, people cheerfully called an 'accident'.

Nowadays, children are often made to feel like their existence is God-decreed, destined by fate and foretold by mystical signs. Nowadays, telling a child that they are the result of a birth-control device failing would be considered potentially damaging to their self-esteem. In contrast, back in my day, it wasn't unusual to name a child after the birth-control device that failed.

Anyway, I won't talk too much about my brother's conception. Unlike millennials who probably sit around with their parents watching videos of the event, we Generation Xers don't typically dwell on it. However, I *can* tell you that I was on a school tour in Dublin with my class when my mother went into labour.

I don't remember what the main event of the school trip was – possibly the zoo or the natural history museum, or just the joy of seeing three-storey buildings – but at some point we went on a lunch break to St Stephen's Green. That's when I decided to climb up the slidey part of a slide rather than using the ladder. I believe I was the first person ever to do this. Nowadays, talent spotters would probably note my disruptive abilities and give me a business grant and a subsidized office in a digital hub. Unfortunately, like many innovators, I flew too close to the sun and thus became a cautionary tale of incorrect slide use. 'Your uncle Patrick broke his arm by doing that,' my mother says regularly to her grandchildren. (They usually ask about the nature of the break and whether you could see the bone, because children are monsters.)

What my mother says is true. As I approached the top of the slide, a smaller-minded but larger-bodied boy decided to slide down the so-called 'correct' way, thus knocking me a) up into the air, b) on to the concrete surface below and c) into the story of my brother's birth.

This was a time before council authorities invested in soft playground surfaces. Back then, it was believed that any injuries earned by children while misusing the facilities were good enough for them.

In fact, I'm pretty sure departmental documents on playground safety statistics in 1981 had titles like 'Good Enough for Them', 'Fourteen Brats Who Got Their Comeuppance' and 'That'll Put a Halt to Their Gallop'.

So my right wrist cracked and my chin was split open, spraying blood everywhere. I did not accept my fate stoically and I proceeded to cry and wail.

'Yes, that's definitely broken,' observed a passing business-man, who, while not necessarily the greatest mind of his generation, was still on hand to mansplain childhood injuries to my panicking teacher and to help her hail a taxi to hospital.

My mother was now in labour, so my father was forced to spend the next twenty-four hours rushing from her side to mine. He proceeded to take charge. My dad is good at taking charge, but these events must have been a challenge even for him.

After my broken bone was put back in place and X-rayed, for example, the doctor said, 'Well, it's not perfect. Do you want it perfect?'

To which my father said, 'Of course I fucking want it perfect.'

So, eventually my arm would have to be rebroken and set again, which is probably why I can type this.

Over in the maternity hospital, my brother had been born. But during one of my father's visits to my bedside, he disappeared. Why he disappeared is a mystery, but I've often thought he did it on purpose in order to reclaim the atten-tion being lavished upon me. Frankly, who knows what was going through his infant mind.

His absence initially went unnoticed until my mother, in a ward filled with women not yet ready to give birth, asked to see her new baby, whom she had met only briefly several hours before.

'You haven't had a baby!' said the ward sister with a pitying voice. 'None of the women here have had babies yet.'

In 1980s Ireland, if a nurse or a nun told you that you didn't have a baby, it was usually considered better to just go with it, so I'm sure my mother was tempted to do just that. But to her credit, she didn't let it lie and decided to ask for her baby once more.*

So insistent was she that she had definitely recently given birth to a baby that some genius decided to look under the blankets. They pressed on my mother's stomach and concluded that she had indeed given birth and that she was in the wrong ward, so they quickly brought her to the nearest post-natal ward, where, they assured her, they would find her baby.

It was a smoking ward, so the idyllic sight of all those new mothers breastfeeding with fags in their mouths must have had her gasping for both a baby and a cigarette (she insists on pointing out that she didn't smoke, so she was just gasping for the baby). Sadly, her baby was not in this ward either.

'Where *is* your baby?' the ward nurse asked then. She did so in an accusing fashion, as though my mother had stashed it somewhere as a hilarious prank, and that's when, amid the stench of fags and baby puke, my mother started to cry.

* It's amazing what you can turn into a 'funny story'. In reality, this must have been absolutely terrifying for my mother. In Ireland in the 1980s, state-funded Catholic institutions were literally trading in the babies of poor women and their hierarchies were not to be questioned.

The nurses quickly left her side to, presumably, panic, search for unclaimed babies and update their CVs. There had recently been a case in which a baby had been abducted from a maternity hospital before being found, unharmed, on the Holyhead–London train. This was fresh in everyone's mind.

So my mother lay there getting increasingly upset until eventually my father arrived back with me in tow and railed profanely at the staff until I'm pretty certain my mother wasn't the only person in the ward crying.

And then something happened.

A baby was produced.

'We're not certain it's the right one,' I imagine they said. 'Do you want the right one?'

My father is a very practical man with an eye for a bargain, so if the doctor had offered him a better baby, I'm sure he'd have rolled with it.

What the nurse *actually* said to my parents when she wheeled a generic infant into the ward was: 'Is this your baby?'

This is a difficult question for even the most loving of parents, because, as my mother points out, all newborn babies look exactly the same; he didn't have any facial tattoos or a moustache, and, as I said, she had only met him briefly a few hours before.

'I guess so?' said my parents.

And so they got a baby.

Nowadays, this traumatic event would probably have led to a very lucrative lawsuit, but in those days the height of my parents' ambition was to get my mother into a private room. This was very gentle revenge, given that their insurance policy had promised a private room anyway. Sadly, it didn't happen. The otherworldly gynaecologist, who hadn't bothered turning up to the birth, wafted in and said: 'A room? One is not a builder.' He really said this.

Meanwhile, I was ignorant of all this drama. I had spent a lovely day in a different hospital enjoying a big bag of Maltesers, a fizzy drink, painkillers and a pile of British war comics, and now I was outside in the corridor with nurses stopping every few minutes to admire my cast. I was having a great time, and even though I hadn't broken my arm on purpose (I'm almost certain of this), it was nonetheless clear now that my parents loved me the most and that I was the best boy.

And so it remains to this day.

The baby my father demanded from the hospital was introduced to me later that day as my brother. I wasn't that impressed. I'd learned a bit about babies since the birth of my sister, who, as a typical middle child, had nothing to do with the dramas I'm recounting here. She was off being untroublesome and possibly even *helpful* in the home of a neighbour while my bones were being set and my brother was, for his own reasons, trying to get as far away from us as possible.

When my sister was born, four years earlier without any such melodrama, I overexcitedly assumed I had gained an instant new playmate, only to learn that babies were rubbish at playing and that she would not be joining me on the green across the road for another couple of years. Frankly, I felt like a prize fool. So, this time, I greeted my new sibling with a shrug.

For years, he looked nothing like me, which must have been worrying for my parents, given the murky circumstances I've described above. They say that they had plenty of other things to be worrying about, what with the recession and the high marginal rate of tax.

Now it's clear that he probably is my brother, although I'll certainly raise all of this again if there's ever a will to be quibbled over. We look remarkably similar these days. This came as a bit of a shock to me as we aged. When he started adopting my gait and speaking style in his teens, I assumed he was just copying me and I found it annoying. Nowadays, old friends, who haven't seen what seven years can do to a man, mistake him for me on the street and my mother can't tell us apart on the phone.

'Get your own style of head!' I say to him. 'Get your own speaking voice. Stop making me look like a "before" picture at a gym.'

'You broke your wrist to steal my thunder *on the day of my birth*,' he says.

I just sigh. He still thinks he's the most important part of this story.

Something Else

In my dream, there has been some unspecified cataclysm and I'm in a strange country. The landscape is sun-scorched and the sea has risen. Large areas are flooded and people are on the move. There are soldiers everywhere and I'm among a trail of refugees who are being moved from a town, which may be my town, Dublin, but which has been left unrecognizably desolated. We're being moved to somewhere safer, somewhere that has more resources.

Here's an important point: I'm with my three-year-old nephew, who I am babysitting a lot at this time. I don't know where the rest of our family are – my wife or my nephew's parents or my parents or anyone else.

My nephew walks for small stretches and I carry him the rest of the time. At some point I find a cart and I pull him along in it. There are no superheroics. There is no dramatic action. We see soldiers from time to time, with rifles on their shoulders, but they just look beaten and tired. We sit at campfires with other refugees. We befriend an older woman and she joins us. My nephew plays with other ragged children and I play with my nephew. I have to search in the ruins of old buildings for scraps of fabric to make nappies with, but there doesn't seem to be a shortage of food. Wherever we go, I ask people about my wife and my nephew's parents, but nobody has seen them. I never meet anyone I know.

We finally arrive at a different town, a seaside town. There are boats and buildings, but the boats all have sails and the buildings seem to be jerry-rigged out of salvaged planks and bits of rubbish. I find a kind of hut built from old crates and blue plastic and decide we should live in it. And it's when lying there, with my nephew asleep on my chest, that I realize that we are never going to find the rest of our family. And I realize something else. I realize that I am his parent now and I am overwhelmed with a feeling of complete and utter happiness.

When I woke from this dream, I was smiling. I had a physical feeling of contentedness, a feeling that stayed with me for the rest of the day and that I can even conjure up a little as I sit here typing this. If most dreams are a surrealistic fog, this was a high-definition, wide-screen production with an unusual amount of narrative coherence. It felt like it *meant* something. I woke up feeling rewired, like my brain chemistry had been changed, like I'd downloaded an upgrade as I slept.

It was still just a dream. There was a certain amount of dream logic going on. I mean, I'm pretty certain that in real life I'd be a lot more upset about the possibly horrific deaths of my wife and my family than I am in this dream. I'm also pretty sure I wouldn't stop searching for them so easily and that I wouldn't just see the end times as a great opportunity to snap up a bargain-basement orphan. And, for the record, for any parents I know who are reading this, I'm not going to leave you for dead and take your baby when the opportunity presents itself. Probably.

But the subtext of the dream is also clear. For a while there I felt hungry to have a child. The hunger peaked at around the time I had realized that it wasn't likely to happen, and my dreams, this one being the most vivid example, reflected that realization.

I had several other dreams involving children. In one, I found a tiny baby in my garden. This baby was so small that I could hold him in the palm of my hand. I sought help for this tiny child, but nobody offered to take him from me or to help me work out where he had come from. I realized that I had to look after him myself and I tried to feed and nurture him, terrified the whole time that I was going to accidentally cause him pain. In another dream, I saw feral babies, newly born, running on all fours up a ravaged mountainside. I woke from those dreams feeling more troubled than happy.

It wasn't just my dreams. At work in the *Irish Times*, I actively sought out pieces to write about child welfare and children's rights. All the short stories I tried to write seemed, when I reread them, to be about parenthood – they were a mass of demonic fathers and ghost mothers. You name a fantastical trope, and I used it as a weird metaphor for surrogate parenthood.

It was all built on something very real. Whenever I saw one of my nephews or my niece clamber on to the lap of their mother or father, I felt a pull on my heart. Sometimes it felt like an actual punch in the chest. Sometimes it felt like a real physical need.

Did I always want to be a parent? All the images of the future that I conjured when I was younger were vague and riddled with fantasy. I had daydreams, but I don't think I ever had plans. I had at different times envisaged my future self as a soulful crime fighter or as an acclaimed and wealthy musician or a valued member of an anarchist commune somewhere in Europe. None of these scenarios saw me moving beyond my thirties. My fantasies involved freedom, moral certainty and companionship, but none of them featured children.

And yet, as I got older, it slowly dawned on me that I'd always assumed that I'd have kids. I did so in the way that I always assumed that someday I would be grey-haired and that someday I would die. It was the default option. And then, as the years went by, I realized it was not the default. One day I looked around and everyone seemed to have children and we – Anna and I – did not.

Now, there's more to our story than I'm going to write about here. But the short version is: we are people who love children but for whom having them would be complicated. We didn't go down difficult paths like IVF or adoption. We would have liked to be parents, but maybe there were limits to how much we were willing to do. It's complicated. (It's always complicated.)

I've done everything else I was supposed to do in life, more or less – school, college, work, marriage, home ownership. Over these years, there were times when I thought I was out of step with my peers, when I was too slow to achieve some of these things or was too cynical about them.

In fact, I was still marching in time, I was just slightly syn-copated. When you *really* fall out of step with your generation, you know it. You realize that your previous rebellions were minor things, colourful and entertaining little deviations. You were secretly conforming all along.

Not having kids is the big deviation. We're *meant* to have children. Society is geared towards it and there are plenty of people out there keen to reinforce the norms and remind you of them.

'You should really have kids,' a colleague said, as though this thought had never occurred to me.

'*When* you have children . . .' someone else said, as though birth control and feminism never happened.

'As a parent, I really feel for the victims of this disaster,' say other people. (Are these people such psychopaths that they needed to reproduce before they could feel empathy?)

Against this backdrop of thoughtless busybodies, I've thought a lot about parenthood. Firstly, none of us need to have kids nowadays. We don't need to have them to look after us in old age or to tend to our farms or simply as an automatic consequence of having a sex life. Having children, for relatively privileged people, is a choice and a statement of robust self-worth. After great consideration, these parents have concluded: 'You know what the world needs? More of *me*!'

And let's not make any mistake about it, parenthood doesn't make people better. I've seen parents whose love for their children has curdled into fear and distrust of the wider world. I've seen humans brought into existence so people

can re-enact their damaged family dynamics. And sometimes the great love the parents hoped to feel for their kids
never arrives. That's why therapists exist – for all those
wounded former children of wounded former children. The
history of psychoanalysis is basically 'the case against keeping this going'.

And against all this, childless people are often repre-
sented as selfish. But you can't fool me. I wanted to be a
parent enough to know that parenthood is intensely selfish,
built on a desire, not just to love but to *be* loved. We remember the intensity of the love we felt for our parents when we
were children. I could distinguish my father's footsteps in a
distant corridor and pick out my mother's scent in a crowded
room. I worried about them. I wanted to please them. It's
the child's love that's really unconditional, not the adult's.
Ask any therapist. Who doesn't want to feel that childlike
love? We have a postcard on our fridge written to us from
Spain by our nephew when he was six. 'I love Anna and
Patrick,' he wrote, all the 'a's written backwards. I sometimes
stop when I'm passing the fridge just to look at it. I can feel
the love radiating from it.

And yes, I know that many people feel something deep,
something in their guts and in their marrow – a want that's
primal. I know that feeling too. I know it from the times
sleepy toddlers have nuzzled their hot faces into my shoulder. I know it from the times that small hands have pushed
themselves into mine at traffic lights. And I know it from
the dream I recounted at the start of this essay.

I like being an uncle and a godfather. I like feeding

children and I like putting them to bed and I like talking to them. I particularly like childish insults, though, it has to be said, children are better at it and it's madness to think you can keep up. Recently at the playground, a familial battle of wits culminated in one small nephew gleefully shouting at my fellow uncle, Aaron, that he was 'a bum man who likes bums and sells bums all day'. The worst swearword he knows is bum. Let me just say, if you have to shout, 'I'm *not* a bum man who likes bums and sells bums all day!' at a five-year-old in a children's playground, you're losing.

This is all a long way of saying that if the vague disaster in that dream comes to pass, there are plenty of children I know and like who I will endeavour to enlist into my post-apocalyptic entourage.

There's Cillian, who has a series of huge photographic portraits of himself aged one that make him look like he's hosting a late-night talk show called *Modern Baby*.

There's Senan, who as a toddler was found to be awake in the night, standing staring at the moon with his hands behind his back like an evil genius.

There's Etain, who enlisted some schoolfriends in a ruse to knock out one of her teeth in order to get money for the tooth fairy. The friends were instructed to make it look like an accident, prison yard-style.

There's Stanley, who reminds me of Richmal Compton's self-serious William Brown, and Frank, who likes to gas-light adults with fake news, and Holly, who is very young and waves 'bye bye' at me as soon as I arrive at her house. ('Bye bye', if you don't speak baby, means 'fuck off'.)

There's Gilles, whose father works for Samsung and who responded to his mother's desire for an iPhone with an appalled: 'But we are a Samsung house!'

There's Eli and Arlo, who perform long, elaborately choreographed performances to Spotify playlists. They call this 'the Finale', and I'm pretty sure I could make it into some sort of post-apocalyptic revue if all goes well.

Yes, I could, if I wished, gather a child army if the apocalypse were to come and their parents were to disappear. And I think I would be a good Faginesque father figure. I think I might have even made a good parent in the real world. In my daydreams about this, I'm certainly very caring and very wise.

At my most vulnerable, I worry that being without children makes me an unimportant non-person. I worry that I'm going to get weird, that not having a feedback loop of care with a smaller human is going to cause my heart and soul to shrivel up. I worry that we were put here on Earth to be people-makers and that if I don't get on with that task I'll lose my membership card for the human race. And I worry that having children grants people access to some big secret that's denied to the rest of us.

Without kids, the future looks simultaneously more open and more daunting. I go over and back on this. Right now, when I think about Anna and I making our own kind of future, not shaped by other people's expectations or fitted to the life cycle of younger humans, I feel lucky. Who is to say how any of this pans out, after all? The writer Elizabeth Gilbert once said that you don't always get what you want, but you do get something else.

One of the things I got was the weird dream that prompted this essay and which I still think about a lot. The clear message I should have taken from it, if I had been paying attention and not caught in a fog of baby-want, is that this destroyed world is *not* one to have a child in. If that dream was significant in any mystical way, it's as a warning. Yet somehow my brain turned it into a heart-warming story about acquiring a second-hand child and retiring to live in a shed. If there's a Part Two rattling about in my subconscious, it certainly involves the child eating me. Which, yes, I know, is also a metaphor for parenthood.

So I've changed my mind about that dream and what it's about. I now think it was a dream about love and what we do with love. I still feel sad about this stuff from time to time. I've thought in the past that it was a sort of grief that I'd been recovering from. But as I feel more optimistic about things, I'd amend that. I've experienced grief and this is not it. This is a type of love, a type of love I now hope to put to use elsewhere. It's OK, folks, nobody died. We all get something else.

Stories about Driving

Paul got the camper van from a dealer in second-hand camper vans somewhere on the German–Polish border.

'It looks legit,' he said, which is a sentence no one says about anything that looks entirely legit.

His trip to fetch the camper van, spotted on a website, did not go completely as planned. It started with him misplacing his passport somewhere between Dublin and London and having to get an emergency one organized in the small hours of the morning by a civil-servant friend based in Knightsbridge. This young man lived in a beautiful government-leased high-ceilinged apartment which we sporadically filled with guitars and cigarette smoke and from which I once, in bafflement, watched an older, wealthier neighbour doing t'ai chi. This civil-servant friend was one of many people we took for granted over the course of our low-key, high-stakes rock career.

With Paul's passport sorted, he flew on to Germany and bought the camper van, which he then had to drive all the way back to Ireland. He had to do this in twenty hours because the band had a very special gig.

Why was it a special gig? I can't believe you asked that. They are *all* special gigs.

That night we were supporting a low-profile American

rockabilly band you have never heard of and that I have already forgotten in a minor venue in Dún Laoghaire. It was *clearly* a very important gig.

Paul drove from Germany without stopping except to fill the van with petrol and to fill his stomach with coffee and arrived at Dún Laoghaire with moments to spare. He didn't look entirely sure that he had arrived. He stumbled out of the camper blinking in the waning sunlight as I tapped my watch theatrically.

'I'm here?' he said, and we could hear the question mark at the end.

He was deranged with lack of sleep. At a certain point while driving, he told us, he began seeing a little boy run across the road in front of him. The little boy did this again and again. The boy was chasing a ball. After swerving to avoid this ball-chasing boy many times, he realized the little boy wasn't real. So, he stopped swerving and just drove through him. Eventually, the boy was accompanied by ninjas, he said. He drove through the ninjas too.

He told us this story because he wanted us to congratulate him on how clever he was. He had figured out how to drive while hallucinating. It never occurred to any of us that the correct response to hallucinating while driving is to stop driving and to sleep, not to learn how to correctly recognize hallucinations.

So, yes, we congratulated him. Because the alternative option was believing that not being involved in a horrific motorway accident was more important than potentially missing a gig in Dún Laoghaire with a minor American indie band.

Why did we think like this?

'Because they are all special gigs.'

Well done. Now you get it.

I drive a lot for work nowadays, as a journalist, but usually on my own and usually to some place where I have to make strangers have conversations with me. It's a lonely and sometimes existentially troubling job that I do without a band to bolster me. And yet, due to some psychic hangover from those early days, I still love driving through the outskirts of cities.

I like the warehouse buildings and the wholesalers and the industrial estates and the big showrooms that sell kitchen counters. I like the glow of the petrol stations and the promise of the drive-through takeaways and the truck stops and the service stations that are always laid out in the same way. I like the light poles and the big metal signs and the painted road patterns and the flyovers and the ways that all of those things curve off in different directions at different speeds depending on tricks of perspective and light as I drive through. I like to imagine what future aliens will make of all these weird metal and concrete artefacts. I think about journeys I've taken in the past. I think about journeys I will take in the future. I wonder, vaguely, if it's possible to be buried in a place like that. Yes, I'd like to be buried where the industrial estates meet the outer suburbs. Sometimes I imagine that I'm dead already and that this is limbo. It's not so bad.

My friend E, another writer, tells me I like 'liminal

spaces'. Which, I think, means that I like marginal, in-betweeny things. This is true, but the reality is that I also like these areas because they suggest safety and comfort and normality. Nowhere with operating kitchen showrooms and office parks is currently being bombarded or starved of food supplies and, deep down, I am a practical member of the bourgeoisie who respects this. And I like these areas because being near them usually means a journey is either ending or beginning. One possibility gives me hope. The other relief, I guess.

The camper was off-white and cream and yellow, all the best colours, and its steering wheel was on the left. There was a little table behind the driver's cab on which we ate dinner and played cards, and there was a toilet at the back which we were forbidden to use for its intended purpose – it wasn't set up right – and where we stored gear. This was a home away from home, albeit a home without a working toilet. It was a headquarters. It was a hotel. It was a place to have band meet-ings at which we all wielded big hardback notebooks and scribbled notes in different-coloured pens. We were music-industry professionals and behaved accordingly.

The van wasn't the only expensive thing we bought with band funds. We purchased a Fender Rhodes electric piano and speaker which we collected from one of the Ballymun towers several years before those towers came tumbling down. It belonged to a man who left the country in the sev-enties and never returned, a story that intrigues me now but flew over my head at the time. It had been taking up space in his sister's flat and it had to come down the stairs because the lift wasn't working. It cost us three hundred pounds. The Fender Rhodes was too big and heavy to bring to gigs in our hatchback cars, which suited Paul and me just fine. 'We can use the Casio,' said Paul, because, in fairness, we could use the Casio.

'But now we have the van,' said D, the bass player, who likes things to look well, and while the Rhodes was insanely heavy, it did look well. So now that we had the camper van we had to lug the Rhodes to every gig. The van also meant we had no excuse for not bringing anyone who wanted to tag along to gigs with us. 'Now we have the van,' we said a lot.

I only learned to drive because otherwise we would have to be driven to and from gigs by our dads, and that's not a great look for any band.

The first time I ever drove on my own, I drove my mother's car from Newbridge to Portlaoise and back in the dark without any lights on. I didn't notice this mistake at the time. Afterwards, I realized I'd turned on the rear windshield wipers instead of the headlights, which meant that if the worst had come to the worst, at least my rear window would have been impressively clean when the paramedics came. The paramedics did not need to come. I was guided home, instead, by the angry car horns of other vehicles and my own apparently incredibly good night vision.

Unsurprisingly, it took me several years and multiple attempts to pass the driving test. The first time I did it, the tester actually reached over and grabbed the steering wheel at one point because he was scared.

Our initial band vehicles were hatchback cars. Mine was a maroon Opal Corsa that had its own damp microclimate and a persistent mould that probably deserved study. I loved this car. It was basically a cube, and I became obsessed with the art of filling it with musical equipment. I could fit two guitars, a drum kit, two amplifiers and three people within, as long as we placed the smallest person (D) in the back seat, wedged against amps and in serious danger of being skewered by a loose drum stand. I was inordinately proud of my packing skills and offered to demonstrate them a lot. Nobody was as impressed by this as you might expect.

As our entourage expanded – extra guitarists, road managers, sound engineers, support acts – we started to take two hatchbacks out on the road. We toured the UK this way several times. Twice we brought our friend Ian with us, because he had his own van that he used for a fledgling tiling business. It did not look like a van for a fledgling tiling business. It was a hearse formerly owned by a local eccentric who had purchased it for his amateur embalming business. It did not look like a hearse for an amateur embalming business. The amateur embalmer had fitted it out with hydraulic suspension and American-style police lights and a siren. The local eccentric, I can only suppose, wanted to look like a US police embalmer.

A bouncing police-hearse with potentially illegal sirens was not the ideal van to be driving around Britain's motorways. It was stopped first by customs officials on the way through Holyhead, who wanted to see Ian's driving licence. Ian only had a provisional driving licence, which wasn't permitted on UK motorways.

'Oh, in Ireland we're allowed to drive anywhere with that,' he lied to the customs men.

At first they seemed ready to believe anything of our post-colonial backwater, but one of them thought to ring the Irish Department of Transport to check, and rushed off to do so.

'Is that true?' asked D. 'Can you really drive on that licence?'

'Sure,' lied Ian.

The customs man couldn't get through to the Department of Transport. Ian surmised that the customs man hadn't been able to get through because it was the day after Ireland's first match at the 2002 World Cup. 'Nobody in Ireland goes to work after a World Cup match,' he said.

The customs men believed him. They were unsure what to do after this, so they stood around lamenting the state of Irish traffic legislation for a while before letting us drive through.

A week later, on the way back, the customs men asked Ian to open the back of his quasi-police car/hearse so they could search it.

'I can't do that,' said Ian.

'Open the van,' said the customs people.

'I can't do that,' said Ian.

'Open the van,' said the increasingly aggravated customs people.

'I can't do that,' said Ian again, acting, as far as the aggravated customs people were concerned, like international drug mogul Pablo Escobar (if Pablo Escobar drove around in a modified police car/hearse).

Ian literally couldn't do that because the back door of the hearse was broken, but he was interminably slow at explaining this. In order to open the door over the preceding week, Ian had had to crawl across the amps and drum paraphernalia in the dark before kicking the door open with his boot. You know, just like Bono has to do with his van. The customs men looked very tired when they were talking to Ian.

Sometimes I find myself on car journeys with my mother, to see family down in the south of the country or to go to a hospital appointment. 'You're a very good driver,' she always says. She says this because she's a nurturing baby boomer who believes in the importance of encouraging her middle-aged infant.

She thinks I'm a very good driver only because she has seen other members of the family drive. Those nameless family members zip in and out of traffic and drive right up to the bumper of other cars in the fast lane and they mutter curse words and shake their fists. If they had guns – and at least one of them formerly had access to guns – they would fire them out the window as they drove instead of using the car horn or the headlights.

Yet, my mother probably praises them too. 'It's very impressive how you terrified that young woman in that Fiat,'

I imagine her saying. 'She'll certainly think twice before coming out on the road again.'

I really enjoy my journeys with my mother. I quite enjoy driving when I'm in no hurry and I can amble along the roads, chatting. But I'm not sure I really am a good driver. I don't drive particularly recklessly and I give people space, but I also daydream. I have, at least once, fallen asleep while driving. I am also very easily spooked when someone in the passenger seat suggests an alternative route. Once spooked, I hit kerbs and I veer over yellow lines and I end up having to stop at a service station for a coffee to steady my nerves.

'OK,' my passenger usually says with a sigh. 'We'll go the way you know.'

One day I woke up midway between Galway and Dublin to find the camper van filled with the gentle sound of snoring. It was a comforting sound that seemed to come from all parts of the van at once. My eyes tried to focus and I saw spotlights illuminating the white line in the darkness ahead.

I started to work things out. Where was I? A car or van of some kind. What part of the van? The passenger seat. What time was it? It was night-time. Was the van in motion? Yes, it was. Where was the source of these snores? Why, it was Paul.

I screamed.

'I only dozed off for a second,' said Paul, who was also, I should mention, the driver.

'You can't sleep when you're driving,' I scolded, as though he had done this on purpose just to annoy me.

'But it's your job to keep me awake,' he said, which was also true.

Falling asleep is a hazard of night driving. A few years later another musician friend woke up upside down in his car in a field after finishing a gig an hour or so earlier in Galway. He was, thankfully, unhurt. He was helped from his upturned car by the estranged husband of a minor television celebrity. Then, in the darkness, the two of them loaded his musical equipment from the wreck of his very old car and placed it into the celebrity spouse's four-wheel-drive jeep.

I wonder what they talked about as they drove towards Dublin? There's an accelerated intimacy that happens when people share a journey together. I find it amazing to this day. Maybe it's some sort of tribal memory of a time when all journeys took weeks and bonding with your travelling companions was important for survival. Maybe it's just the flipside of the reduced empathy that turns all pedestrians into soulless targets for a driver's road rage. One way or another, every time we had another musician in the car or van with us, I overshared. I did this no matter how little I knew them. I told them things about my life. I told them about my fears. I invited them to meet my family. I asked them their opinions about medical issues. I suggested we go on holidays together. I told them all about the fights I was having with the rest of my band and asked for advice. I tried to enlist them on my side of the argument: 'Isn't D being unreasonable about the Fender Rhodes?'

I usually never saw these people again. I cringe, thinking

about these moments, but it still happens whenever I'm giving someone a lift. If you want me to marry one of your more wayward siblings or to leave you some money in my will, or need an investor for a crazy scheme, then book some time beside me in the passenger seat of a car.

On the other hand, I loved being on tour with my actual friends – my band, our partners, our friends' bands. For a worried young man fearful of rejection, there is something relaxing about having your friends trapped with you in a tight metal space from which they can't escape.

We toured on a budget. We were not with a label. We were often on the dole. And yet, somehow, going on a tour of Britain while on social welfare seemed like a good idea by the time D had finished outlining the maths in his ledger. This is a *good* decision, we'd think.

We survived because we were thrifty. We arrived into venues from Wrexham to Brighton in our white suits and embroidered jeans and rat's tails and cowboy hats and handlebar moustaches and with a cooler filled with food bought at budget supermarkets. We talked about 'salad' a lot, which one promoter assumed was a slang term for drugs until D started tossing a salad near the sound desk.

Supporting some major-label compatriots in a tiny club in Exeter, we were surprised by the sight of a huge tour bus blocking the street outside as we pulled up alongside it in our wagon train of hatchbacks.

'We heard through the grapevine that we're going to get dropped from the label,' said the singer. 'So we decided to waste as much of their money as we possibly could.'

I was very impressed by this greedy fatalism. I walked the length of their tour bus in a state of envious awe. There was a big television, and bunks with curtains on them. This was not only a far superior form of transport to our own, it was also a far superior form of accommodation: we slept on the floors of local promoters, for the most part. On one occasion I wandered a house in Cardiff at two in the morning trying to find somewhere to lie down that wasn't sticky. On another we had to share a sitting room with a man who spent the whole night watching the *Big Brother* live feed. Sometimes, in Holiday Inns, we slept five to a bed.

When I was small and easily frightened, my family would regularly travel late at night from my grandparents' farm in Kilkenny through winding roads and darkened fields to our home in Kildare. I hated looking out of the window then because I had a vivid imagination and was terrified of seeing something inexplicable and strange in that darkness. Even now, when I drive at night I believe there is something uncanny out there waiting for me. In those days, I would close my eyes and think about more explicable things, like my cousins or toys that I wanted to own. This isn't possible now if I want to arrive at my destination in one piece. In those days, I usually fell asleep before arriving home and then I would be lifted into my bed by my dad. Being carried to bed by my father made me feel safe. Probably safer than I've ever felt since.

*

Several years after we stopped our endless touring, I whispered to Paul, 'I'm glad we never became successful.'

He looked around as though about to say something sacrilegious and whispered back: 'Me too.'

There were a number of reasons we had seen the light. I had, by this point, spent time with a number of touring Americana bands. These consisted largely of wise, seasoned musicians, usually heading past forty. They didn't drink so much any more and they were very kind with their advice to younger musicians, but they seemed weary. They could be heard worrying about finances and sighing when they saw low ticket sales. Their lives didn't look like that much fun. These bands were trapped by the decisions made by younger versions of themselves. They were now too small to tour in comfort and too big to quit. That, at best, was our future trajectory as a band.

And here's the thing: we were never very rock 'n' roll people. I liked being in bed early. I liked a steady income. I no longer enjoyed filling cars with amplifiers. I wanted to be able to meet my bandmates, my best friends, for coffee with no band business to discuss.

I have a theory that everyone has a *natural* age and the nature of their dysfunction at any point in life is based on how near or far they are from that age. For some, their natural age is exactly nineteen and their life ever since has been a disappointing descent from that hedonistic bliss. I have always felt that my natural age was around forty-four. I love cardigans and slippers and safety and books by the fire. I am forty-four now.

Paul never saw forty-four. In the week after his death I tried to be useful. So I did what I always did: I played music and I drove. I played music at the funeral and spent a few days driving people who had come for the funeral around the city. Then one morning, when it was over, I found I couldn't get out of bed and stayed there for twenty-four hours thinking of hatchbacks and camper vans and Paul.

At two in the morning, off the motorway somewhere between Cork and Dublin, Paul woke me. He had a problem, he said. He couldn't open the petrol tank on the camper van and we really needed petrol. He wasn't sure of the science of it, he said, but he was pretty sure the van needed petrol to make it go.

He had already tried unsuccessfully to wake D. D is a practical man, but he was very wedded to the idea of a good night's sleep and as a non-driver he saw the camper van as our domain. There were other people sleeping in the camper too, people I love, but let's not beat around the bush here: when it came to practical concerns, they were fools.

So I got up and, blinking in the light of a petrol-station forecourt, I slapped my hands together like I've seen more practical men do. I found that what Paul had said was true: the cap of the petrol tank felt almost welded shut. With a big effort, I wrenched the plastic external casing of the petrol cap off the van entirely. This left the metal internal casing lodged in the passage that, under more normal circumstances, brought petrol to the engine.

'Oh no,' I said.

'I knew that was going to happen,' said Paul, unhelpfully.

But Paul was an optimist. He imagined that he could see a little hole in the obstructed petrol tank and that he'd be able to pump petrol through it if only I would create a funnel with the magazine I was reading, which, not that it's important, was probably *Select* or *The Face*.

'Really?' I said.

'I think it will work,' said Paul, firmly. 'Trust me.'

I didn't trust him. But I did convince myself that this was *my* idea, which is what I often did in lieu of trusting my bandmates. So I carefully crafted a little funnel with my magazine and angled the narrow end of this funnel to where Paul believed he saw a hole in the jagged metal remains of the petrol cap.

Then he started pumping little flurries of petrol into my magazine paper funnel. One of our beloved friends/fools stirred within and stared out the window vacantly. What did he think was happening? He waved, turned around and went back to sleep.

The funnel, despite the effort that had gone into its construction, disintegrated because, well, it was made out of paper. So now there was a wash of petrol streaming through my cupped hands and a picture of Brett Anderson from Suede was affixed to my wrist and a little pool of liquid was forming at my feet.

'I'm not sure this is working,' I said, while Brett Anderson from Suede's mournful eyes judged me and I felt faint due to the petrol fumes. I was pretty sure this had never happened to Brett Anderson from Suede. He might have written songs about sniffing solvents, but he didn't splash about in them.

'Yeah, I think you're right,' said Paul, but he kept pumping petrol anyway, his shoulder to my shoulder, as though he wanted to make completely sure that this was a lost cause before we moved on to plan B. (Plan B was ringing my dad to come and rescue us.)

'What's up?' said the guitar player, who had poked his newly awoken head between our fume-addled heads.

God, I'd love a cigarette, I thought, as I gazed at the lovely Marlboro Light hanging from the guitar player's lip. I stared at it, glowing there in the darkness a half a foot above the gentle stream of petrol that was flowing through my hands and on to my trousers and into a glistening puddle at my feet.

I think of this moment often. I think of it whenever people say, as they occasionally do, 'You had a band and released records and went on tour!? That's amazing! Do you ever imagine what might have been?' And I nod sagely, because I *do* imagine what might have been. First, I imagine this moment in a petrol-station forecourt with petrol streaming through my hands. And then I imagine myself running around on fire and screaming on the edge of the N7. That's what might have been, my friends. Don't let anyone tell you otherwise.

Epilogue

In 1988 my whole family was in a car outside a town called Urlingford on the old two-lane road that, in those days, ran from Cork to Dublin. A driver came out of a side road, nearly hitting another car and then veering across the road into the path of our own. We very nearly died. For some reason it never occurred to me to write about this when I wrote the first draft of this essay.

My mother was driving and my grandmother, who had recently lost her husband, was in the passenger seat. I was in the back seat on the left, behind my grandmother. My sister was in the middle seat and my father, with my brother on his lap, was on the right. I have no idea why my father wasn't driving. When my mother and father were together in the car, he almost always drove. On this day, for some reason, he wasn't driving. Maybe my mother wanted to talk to her mother. Maybe they wanted to talk about my grandfather.

And then a car veered across the path ahead. I closed my eyes at the moment of impact. I heard metal and glass shattering. I hit my face against the front seat and reckoned with the pain of that while I felt our car slide wildly across the road. When the car stopped moving, I could feel blood run down my chin and I heard a loud silence for a long moment before I heard my sister and my brother start to cry. I thought, 'At least *they're* alive,' but I waited for another beat before opening my eyes. Everyone was moving. I had blood pumping from my nose. My father and my sister and my brother seemed to be OK (I later found out that my brother had banged his head quite badly). My mother and grandmother were clearly in a lot of pain.

There was a house nearby and we were brought in there while an ambulance came. My mother couldn't walk, and two people had to support her. My grandmother was very shaken. I sat with her in a small siting room as she clutched my hand and called me a 'brave boy', and a kind woman who lived in the house made us cups of tea.

After a while I went outside and stood with my dad, staring at the wreckage of our car. The front bonnet was compressed to almost nothing beneath a cracked windshield. 'It's hard to believe anyone walked out of that,' my dad said quietly. The man in the other car was unharmed, despite having fallen out of his car on to the road as his car skidded away. This seemed miraculous. My nervous system was jangling.

When the ambulances came we were brought to hospital, where we learned that my mother's knee had been badly broken in the crash. My grandmother had some broken ribs. I had a bruised and bleeding nose, but an X-ray showed that nothing was broken. An army colleague collected my father, my siblings and me from the hospital and, a few nights later, my mother still in hospital, another army friend called around with a bottle of whiskey. We were all very shaken.

My mother needed to have many operations on her knee. It was very painful. She stopped kneeling at Mass. In the following weeks my brother started to have fits in his sleep and was diagnosed with acquired epilepsy. So terrified were people in those days of the word 'epilepsy' that shortly afterwards my father's parents offered to leave us their farm in case my brother was so debilitated he could never work. They didn't know what else to do. My father declined the offer.

Afterwards there were court proceedings. I don't really

know the fine details, but my sister and I were awarded two and a half thousand pounds each. Seven years later I used my money to fund my band's first record. My brother, however, was awarded fifty thousand pounds by the courts because of his epilepsy diagnosis. Years later, after his symptoms had disappeared, I felt like I could have done so much more with that money. This essay could have included a tour bus.

I thought about this crash regularly for many years – and then, apparently, forgot about it to the extent I initially didn't include it in this essay. I do know that the first time I ever shut my eyes and didn't want to open them again was sitting in the back seat of that ruined car, and I know that I imagined that moment every time I shut my eyes for some years afterwards. In that moment, anything could have happened.

Dreams about Paul

A month or so after Paul died, I saw him across an unfamiliar school playground, through a gaggle of uniformed children and strangely watchful grown-ups. He didn't make eye contact. He didn't register my existence in any way. I didn't know what he was doing there. For that matter, I wasn't sure what I was doing there. I tried calling out to him, but I found my mouth couldn't make any sounds loud enough for him to hear. I tried to approach him, but it was hard to get through the crowd and he always seemed to get further away.

After this, I saw Paul regularly enough in my dreams. On distant train platforms. Across busy streets in strange cities. In obscure, hard-to-reach alcoves of familiar cafés. He was always in the distance, too far away from me to communicate with. His face was always slightly turned away, as though he was distracted, and my voice was always weak and hoarse. I could never make myself heard.

Whenever I made my way to where he was, he ended up retreating into the distance, to further streets, to further train platforms, to ever-more-distant cities.

A few years later, in another dream, I was at a house party with a lot of younger people I didn't know, or knew only vaguely. They were attractive and hip, gathered around couches chatting, or lined up against walls with drinks in their hands. Paul was there, but we weren't in the same room. I could see him outside a big sash window, standing in a little yard beneath brightly coloured Christmas lights. He was wearing his familiar old yellow-orange anorak. He had a plastic cup in his hand and was talking to two young women under a sort of canopy. The mannerisms were all Paul – the extravagant hand gestures, the way he tossed his head back to laugh. He didn't see me.

'How is he here?' I asked our friend D.

D seemed embarrassed by my puzzlement. 'Calm down,' he said.

Nobody else at the party was particularly alarmed by Paul's presence. But then, as D pointed out, none of them knew Paul, so they didn't know that he was supposed to be dead.

'Is this real?' I asked D.

'Yes,' said D. 'This is real.'

'Why is this happening?' I asked D.

'I don't know,' he said. 'I'm sure there's a reason.'

I didn't talk to Paul that night. I didn't even approach him. He remained on the other side of that pane of glass, slightly turned away from me, talking to people I didn't know. I sat in a corner feeling confused while D made conversation about the 1980s hardcore scene with a punk girl who had skeleton tattoos.

Several years later I fell asleep and as I slept I got a call from D. 'Paul is back,' he said. It was an exact mirror of the conversation we had had years before when he had called early one morning to say: 'Paul is dead.'

'How?' I asked.

'I don't know,' said D. 'There was some sort of misunderstanding.' That didn't seem likely. I remembered the shock, the wake, the body, the funeral, the sad faces. I remembered his body.

Paul's family invited us out to their home. D and I prepared to go over there. We did what felt natural: we organized a band practice. 'There's a lot of work to do,' said D. If Paul was back, we would, of course, make another album. It didn't matter that D was a psychologist now and that I was a journalist with a nine-to-five job and that we were married and had mortgages. Being in a band was a priority again.

Paul's family home was not as I remembered it. It was surrounded by huge trees and had many, many more outhouses surrounding it than I recalled from the days when we were out there several times a week. For some reason, the family now lived on the top floor of an odd new house in the garden which was accessed via a huge, rickety flight of stairs that ran along the side of the building.

D and I climbed the stairs and entered the kitchen, where we spoke to his parents for a while. They were very glad Paul was back. His mother couldn't stop crying. She was crying with happiness. I was happy, too, but I was very confused.

'How is he alive?' I asked.

'It's complicated,' said Paul's father.

Paul came into the room and hugged me. I must have

looked amazed to see him because he laughed and pointed at the expression on my face. We talked for a long time. I filled him in on my life and on all of the things that had happened while he was gone: the friends who had moved away or had children; the people who had got married; the people who had got divorced. Other people who had died.

I felt like I couldn't ask him where he had been or how it was that we all thought that he was dead. All anyone would say was that there had been some sort of mistake. Paul and I talked for a long time. I don't remember all the details of what we talked about, but it felt good. The old warmth was there. We talked about music and the album we were going to record. We talked about our friendship and how it had some-times been strained towards the end. Paul forgave me for the ways I felt I had let him down, for the things I had spent the past ten years worrying about. I forgave him for dying.

'Is this a dream?' I asked at one point. I was still suspicious.

'No,' said Paul. 'It's not a dream.'

And I knew he was right because nobody ever asks that question in a dream. And I took note of all the details – the crack in the windowpane, the spider web in the corner of the room, the feeling of dust in the air as I sucked it into my lungs. This was not a dream, I thought. This was happening. This was a real thing that was happening. My friend had returned and we were young and in a band and it felt so good to have him back and to be there with him, just talking. We had a really good talk that night. I never saw him again.

Acknowledgements

'Let's Do Your Stupid Idea' is one of the philosophies I live by and about which I'm evangelical. Seriously, I'll button-hole you at a party and tell you all about it. It's a mixture of passive aggression and radical openness. It's perfect for working with other people and thriving in your workplace, band or family unit. I used to fight things I thought were stupid ideas. But here's the thing: it takes *a lot* of energy to fight a stupid idea. It usually takes up a lot less time just to *try* the stupid idea.

So, if after you present your misgivings about the invariably stupid ideas of your colleague, loved one or bass-guitarist and they nonetheless persist with them, I recommend that you just say inside your head, 'OK, let's do your stupid idea' and get on with it.

Because truly stupid ideas die on their own and sometimes . . . sometimes their stupid idea is not a stupid idea. Sometimes your colleague, loved one or bass-guitarist is on the money. And then (as long as you didn't say, 'OK, let's do your stupid idea' out loud) you can share the acclaim. I had planned to write an essay about all this. But it turns out *that* was a stupid idea. It was a bad essay. It lies bothering me on my hard drive. So, I used it as the title of this book instead.

The book, by the way, was my editor Brendan Barrington's idea. It *wasn't* a stupid idea. He coaxed it out of me bit by bit until, before I knew it, I'd written half of it. Thanks to him for all the care and attention he's given it and thanks to him for publishing 'Brain Fever' in the *Dublin Review*.

Getting Lucy Luck at C&W to be my agent was also not a stupid idea. She's a very good agent and a wise woman.

Thanks to the *Irish Times* for employing me (the jury is out on that idea) and for permission to republish the essay 'How to Make Friends and Influence Nobody', which first appeared in a slightly different form in that paper in 2014. Thanks to all my editors and colleagues there for helping to make me a better writer.

Thanks to my sister Maria and my brother David (who allowed me to tell the story of his birth). They are very good siblings.

Also, thanks to these small relatives and godchildren of varying heights: Cillian, Senan, Etain, Arlo, Eli, Stanley, Frank, Holly and Gilles. They were no help, to be honest, but I do love them. And thanks to their parents.

Thank you very, very much to my own parents, Joan and Walter, who were very kind about the essays in which they appear in this book and who were also very kind about keeping me alive and being hugely supportive for forty-four years. And thanks to my mother's sister Phil, who is a lovely person, and to all of my cousins.

I'd also like to extend a lot of thanks to my friends Ronan Kelly, Sinéad Gleeson, Rosita Boland and Emilie Pine for excellent writing advice and writerly support.

Thanks to Daragh Keogh for sharing, in Paul's words, 'a rich fantasy life' with me for many years. And thanks to all the many brilliant people I've made music with or sung with, including the whole Carey family, the Jordan family, Angeline Morrison, Pól Ó Conghaile, Kevin Connolly, Mark Palmer, Jeremy Smyth, Lesley Keye, Róisín Ingle, Jonny Hobson, Brian Ingle, Simone George and the Unthanks.

Thanks to my oldest friends – Cormac Horan, Diana Perez Garcia, Claire O'Mahony and Quentin Doran O'Reilly – for staying my friends. Some of them appear in this book and have come up with some of the best stupidest ideas I've ever done.

Some names have been changed in this book. With that in mind, thanks to Corncrake for being himself.

And lastly, thank you Anna Carey, my first reader, my singing partner and the person I want to see every day forever.

He just wanted a decent
book to read ...

Not too much to ask, is it? It was in 1935 when Allen Lane, Managing
Director of Bodley Head Publishers, stood on a platform at Exeter railway
station looking for something good to read on his journey back to London.
His choice was limited to popular magazines and poor-quality paperbacks –
the same choice faced every day by the vast majority of readers, few of
whom could afford hardbacks. Lane's disappointment and subsequent anger
at the range of books generally available led him to found a company – and
change the world.

*'We believed in the existence in this country of a vast reading public for intelligent
books at a low price, and staked everything on it'*
Sir Allen Lane, 1902–1970, founder of Penguin Books

The quality paperback had arrived – and not just in bookshops. Lane was
adamant that his Penguins should appear in chain stores and tobacconists,
and should cost no more than a packet of cigarettes.

Reading habits (and cigarette prices) have changed since 1935, but
Penguin still believes in publishing the best books for everybody to
enjoy. We still believe that good design costs no more than bad design,
and we still believe that quality books published passionately and responsibly
make the world a better place.

So wherever you see the little bird – whether it's on a piece of
prize-winning literary fiction or a celebrity autobiography, political tour
de force or historical masterpiece, a serial-killer thriller, reference book,
world classic or a piece of pure escapism – you can bet that it represents
the very best that the genre has to offer.

Whatever you like to read – trust Penguin.